Love, Otto

The Legacy of Anne Frank

Love, Otto
The Legacy of Anne Frank

Cara Wilson

Andrews and McMeel

A Universal Press Syndicate Company

Kansas City

Otto Frank letters or citations by kind permission of
the ANNE FRANK–Fonds, Basel.

A portion of the royalties for this book is being donated
to the Anne Frank House.

Quotations from *The Diary of a Young Girl* by Anne Frank reprinted
by kind permission of Bantam Doubleday Dell in the United States,
and Valentine Mitchell in Canada and Great Britain.

Library of Congress Cataloging-in-Publication Data

Wilson, Cara.
[Correspondence. Selections]
Love, Otto : the legacy of Anne Frank / by Cara Wilson.
        p.   cm.
Consists chiefly of correspondence between the author and Otto Frank.
        ISBN 0-8362-7032-0
1. Frank, Otto, 1889–1980—Correspondence. 2. Jews—Switzerland—
Basel—Correspondence. 3. Holocaust survivors—Switzerland—Basel—
Correspondence. 4. Wilson, Cara—Correspondence. 5. Jews—United
States—Correspondence. 6. Frank, Anne,—1929–1945—Influence.
7. Holocaust, Jewish (1939–1945)—Netherlands—Amsterdam—
Influence. 8. Frank, Anne, 1929–1945. Achterhuis. I. Frank, Otto,
1889–1980. Correspondence. Selections. II. Title.
DS135.S93F738 1995
940.53'18'092—dc20
[B]   94–47201
                                         CIP

First Printing, April 1995
Second Printing, July 1995

In honor of Otto Frank . . . Anne Frank . . .
and my "Two Trees":
Ethan Wilson and Jesse Wilson

In memory of Gizella Sauberman,
My guardian angel.

Contents

A Note to the Reader:

THE LETTERS THAT APPEAR IN THIS BOOK were typeset directly from the originals, so occassionally you will find instances of "creative" spelling, both on Otto's part and mine. I hope that this lends the book an added touch of authenticity, without being too unsettling for the fastidious among you.

Acknowledgments

N OT TOO LONG AGO, I started my life over again in a new place entirely. It was painful and scary and sometimes I wondered if I'd make it. But there was a strange constant—my fax machine kept spitting out encouragement to write this book from my L.A. friend Ted Field. He helped me create the proposal for this book, and he made sure it got in the right hands at Andrews and McMeel. Both he, Colleeny Ferguson, and Stuart Crowner, my other L.A. pals, wouldn't let up on the continuous cheering and encouragement. Some days and nights their faxes would flow endlessly—prodding me on. It was hard to be scared when I was kept so busy moving forward, writing and rewriting the beginnings of this tremendous undertaking. Thank you, dear Ted, Colleen, Stuart, and Kyle for believing in me and this project so tenaciously. And thank you, Donna Martin, vice president and editorial director of Andrews and McMeel, for saying "yes," and being such a wonderful support throughout this journey. And to JuJu Johnson, Donna's incredible assistant, for her unending availability and encouragement.

Massive thanks to Fritzi Frank, my friend—and adopted grandmother. Like her husband, Otto, Fritzi stood by me through all the peaks and valleys of my life, encouraging me to write and finish this book. As she wrote, "I would be glad if you would succeed primarily for your sake, but also because

I would be happy if Otto would be shown to many readers as the wonderful and helpful person he was for many young people."

Special thanks to Miep Gies and Buddy and Bambi Elias for their encouragement and help from the very beginning; to Father John Neiman for his limitless knowledge about Anne and her entire family; to Kent Wilson for pushing me forward toward every adventure in my life, this being the most powerful one. Thank you, dear Buck, for making it possible to meet Otto at long last; Ethan and Jesse for being my sons, the greatest gifts in my life, my true soulmates; my precious parents, Aaron and Lilly Weiss, sweet sister and friend Laura, and Tess, Noah, and Dan Winds-Johnson for your endless support and love; Aunt Rosie, my shelter in the storm, who read my cards and told me years ago this would happen; Marilyn Wilson Proffer, dear spirit-sister, who always encouraged me to do this; Francis Cousens, that gorgeous hunk of a high school teacher who told me I should be a writer; Gary Blum, the kindest friend and lawyer in the world, and wonderful Ellen Feldman, his assistant; Jane and Steve Bello, who answered my millions of contract/publisher questions and opened their hearts and home to me; Seamus Murphy, "911 Computer Genius," always there for me when my computer and I were both on overload; Robertson's Antiques and Art: a safe harbor of love, laughter, and great lunches with Nick Robertson and Cam Wilde; Copies By-The-Sea, owned by Barbara Podoloff, who helped me compile and organize these years of communications into something I could work with; Cappie Baptie, who sent out the lifeboat; Emma Johnson, who kept me in it; and to all the other special souls in my life—that would take pages more to name—my loving friends. You know who you are.

Love, Otto

The Legacy of Anne Frank

℘ 1

Back to the Beginning

THE TRAIN WAS HYPNOTIC. Swaying back and forth, I felt my thoughts lulling into that comfortable state of twilight, zoning out into the past—where this strange pilgrimage first started. Clickety-clickety . . . verdant woods, pastures, quaint cottages, and reed-fringed lakes appeared and vanished as if in a dream. Blink. A gabled roof. Blink. Windswept bridges. Blink. Windmills! Lord. This wasn't a dream. This was Amsterdam. And I was on this train—me, a young mother of two little boys—alone for the first time in my life.

My husband, Kent, and sons, Ethan, age seven, and Jesse, five, were far away in the United States. Kent had encouraged me to do this ever since he'd gone on a business trip to Amsterdam and visited the Anne Frank House. I'd pictured this happening since I was twelve years old. That's when I first discovered Anne Frank, and the wonderful man I grew to love as my own grandfather—Anne's father, Otto.

And here I was, sitting on two huge parcels of luggage, because they were too heavy to drag any further. The train was jammed full with travelers, and I was sweltering from trying to shove my tons of stuff into the third car light-years away. I found a corner and collapsed from exhaustion and the stifling heat. And then the reality hit big-time. My dream was coming true.

It had begun happening very fast just weeks before, with a call I placed from the United States to Otto Frank in Basel, Switzerland, where he had lived for many years.

"Hello, Otto? Is it really you?"

"Cara. Cara! Is this you, Cara?"

His voice, like mine, was filled with emotion. We were speaking for the first time after eighteen years of correspondence.

"Yes, Otto—it's true! If you and Fritzi will be home the last week of July, I'll visit you."

"Cara, I am too nervous to talk further. Here, you must tell Fritzi of these things. We want very much to see you, Cara."

The plan was for me to fly to Amsterdam, where I'd visit the Anne Frank House in the company of Miep Gies, Otto Frank's faithful employee who had sheltered the family and saved Anne's diary, unread, for Otto. And then I would travel by train to Basel to meet Otto himself, my devoted correspondent, along with his beloved Fritzi, the second wife whom he had met as he left the concentration camp.

That call was a beginning to a fulfillment of a dream that had begun to take shape when, at age twelve, growing up in Southern California's San Fernando Valley, I had been chosen by Twentieth Century–Fox film studio to audition for the starring role in the movie *The Diary of Anne Frank*.

I didn't get the part, but by now I had found a whole new world. Anne Frank's diary, which I read and reread, spoke to me and my dilemmas, my anxieties, my secret passions. She felt the way I did. Yet she didn't tell anybody but her diary. In her cramped, secret world of hiding, Anne Frank hid her thoughts, too.

The year was 1957. It was the year that Martin Luther King Jr. formed a group called the Montgomery Improvement Association, which organized a bus boycott in Montgomery, Alabama, that forced a bus company to desegregate. I remember being intensely interested that there was a world outside my comfortable little valley-girl existence. It was a cruel one, very different from my own, and I knew I needed to know more. But I was too involved in being me.

In those days, I was listening to love songs on the radio: Pat Boone crooning "April Love" and "Love Letters in the Sand," and Tab Hunter singing "Young Love." How I wanted to be in love like that. I watched movies—*Bus Stop, Carousel,* and my favorite still, *Bridge on the River Kwai.* Like other girls, I teased and sprayed my hair into one of those loathsome beehive hairdos and dressed in shapeless "sack" dresses, while the guys slicked their hair into "cool" ducktails. How I hated those days. I would look in the mirror and cry. Nothing worked. I was miserable being me.

When I discovered Anne Frank, I was on the brink of that awful abyss of teenagedom and I, too, needed someone to talk to.

My parents were—and still are—loving supports in my life, but I idealized the intense relationship Anne had with her father. (Ironically, Anne, too, expressed a longing for more attention from her father.) My own father was actively involved in the administration side of running a synagogue (the place where the scout picked me to audition for the role of Anne Frank). Dad's whole life was a series of meetings. At home, he was too tired or too frustrated to unload on.

I had something else in common with Anne. We both had to share with sisters who were prettier and smarter than we felt we were.

As a young Jewish girl myself, I identified so strongly with this eloquent girl of my own age, that I now think I sort of became her in my own mind. Her predicament burned in my thoughts: How she stayed in that tiny Dutch annex above her father's spice factory, cramped and bursting with frustrated life, "like a canary in a cage." How she remained hidden for two years in that small space with her parents, Otto and Edith, her older sister, Margot, and another family, the Van Daans, and their son, Peter, and the dentist, Mr. Dussel.

How, after all she had been through, she still believed that "people are really good at heart." She continued, "If I look up to the heavens, I think that it will all come right, and that peace and tranquility will return again."

Despite the monumental differences in our situations, to this day I feel that Anne helped me get through the teens with a sense of inner focus. She spoke for me. She was strong for me. She had so much hope when I was ready to call it quits.

And so Otto became the idealized father figure for me. I imagined, on a distant continent and in a persona I could only fantasize, he would be there for me—as he was for Anne. I could be more vulnerable and open with a "father" so far away. I could turn to Otto for solace.

Two years later, I was able to get Otto's address in Basel from the office of George Stevens, director of the movie *The Diary of Anne Frank*. But would he answer me? Did he speak English? Could I even talk to him of Anne, or would it be too painful? I wrote—and waited.

Then during that hot summer just a few weeks before dreaded school began, an airmail letter from Switzerland was delivered. I must have reread it a hundred times! Somehow it made little difference that he wanted no part of an ongoing correspondence:

August, 21, 1959

I received your kind letter and thank you for it. It was very nice of you to send me your photo, so that I have a better impression of your person. . . . Anne's ardent wish was to work for mankind and therefore an Anne Frank Foundation has been incorporated in Amsterdam to work in her spirit. In the house in which we have been hiding, an International Youth Center will be established and maybe you will be able to visit it and work for it when your plan to come to Europe one day can be realized. You are right that I receive many letters from young people all over the world, but you will understand that it is not possible for me to carry on correspondence, though, as you see, I am answering to everyone.

Wishing you all the best, I am with kindest regards,

Yours, Otto Frank.

I remember answering that he was not to worry, he didn't have to answer me. I recognized his busy schedule. I would simply write to him whether he answered me or not. Well, what choice did the poor man have? Whenever an attack of "I-can't-take-this-any-longer" would hit me, I'd put it all into lengthy diatribes to my distant guru, Otto Frank. It must have all been too intense to ignore, for he would always answer me. Thus, as they say in the movies, began our long friendship. As the traumas of my life arose, he never scoffed nor condescended, but told it straight, as he saw it.

☙ 2

A Teenager in the Sixties

MY COUNTRY WAS heading into one of the most devastating, passionate decades in its history: the sixties. It was marked by peace marches, sometimes-violent protests against the war in Vietnam, and race riots by blacks. Everything seemed to be point-counterpoint: Congress passed the Civil Rights Act of 1960, which addressed voter registration practices. It didn't allow for enforcement of the act, however, so it was essentially ineffective.

And, in contrast to Martin Luther King's Southern Christian Leadership Conference (SCLC), dedicated to nonviolent protest to draw attention to discrimination, another group was born. This was the Student Nonviolent Coordination Committee (SNCC), formed during a lunch counter sit-in in Greensboro, North Carolina. Though it called itself nonviolent, in truth it advocated direct, militant action. The iron fist inside the glove.

Even though I remember being aware of these issues bubbling to the surface in the papers and on TV, the arrogance of my youth was apparent. It took many more years before my letters reflected the pain of the times I was living in. Either I didn't want to face it, or it simply didn't affect me. I was a white teenager, full of hopes and dreams that seemed to me to have every reason to come true.

I lived in a comfortable cocoon. The sixties had an insidious innocence, and I was part of that innocence. I remember the early sixties for the hip action to the tune of Chubby Checker's "The Twist" and Elvis "Pelvis" belting "Are You Lonesome Tonight?"

Some of my early letters to Otto aren't available, but my angst is quite clear in his responses to me. In one instance, I had been railing about sibling rivalry. My younger sister, Laura, was my nemesis. Popular, beautiful, brilliant, she was everything I longed to be. I poured out my heart to Otto, and he responded in turn:

Basel, 6/1959

Well, I just want to say, that it is quite normal, that sisters or brothers quarrel together at times, and so did Margot and Anne. . . . The main thing is to know, that you intend the best, even if opinions differ. Your sister is still very young and so are you. Life is not always gay and I hope that later on, one will be a support for the other in every difficulty which may occur."

His words were true. Laura is my dearest friend today.

It was also during that time that I made Otto some cufflinks. I can't believe I had the gall to consider myself a jeweler, but Otto seemed genuinely pleased. He also talked about a passion of his. He would mention this throughout our correspondence:

June 7, 1960

. . . I am interested in youth all over the world and their problems. For this purpose I stimulated the establishment of the International Youth Center of the

Anne Frank Foundation in Amsterdam with the aim
to foster understanding between young people and to
work with them in Anne's spirit against discrimination
of all kinds.

Years later, I would discover how deeply committed
Otto was to this cause. But now I was fifteen, and thoroughly
involved in me—and my active imagination. I wanted to be
an actress and a dancer and asked Otto what I should do. His
answer made a huge impact on my life:

Basel, 7/1960

As I see you are seriously thinking what to do later,
I appreciate your confidence very much asking my
opinion. I can understand your desire to become an
actress and dancer, but considering all you wrote me I
think, that you should not make this the goal of your
life. Continue to study dancing, continue to work on
literature and drama, but let it be your private hobby.
There are many amateur groups, very good ones too, so
you always will be able to appear on the stage, if you
continue to feel like. But to have acting and dancing as a
job is very different. Even if you are talented, it affords
continuous work from morning to night, you cannot
have a real family life, you must give up privacy. A
famous figure is in the light of the world (like Royalties),
always considering: what will the public say or think of
me. No, I would not wish this for you. I have a nephew,
who is a star in "Holiday on Ice." He is traveling all over
in the world, he has a good time—but he must renounce
to family life. He is more than happy, if he has a vacation
and can stay with us "at home," he cannot marry and

have a home for himself. Many of his colleagues did, but in most cases it is not a success. So I have to join those of your friends who are not in favour of your idea.

From all you wrote I feel that you are a very good hearted girl. You should not worry too much yet about your future. In growing up you certainly will be able to make the right choice.

You ask about my life. I am remarried and we are living here in the same house with my married sister and her family. We have a lot of correspondence and I am busy to organize in Amsterdam an Anne Frank International Youth Center. Therefore we are travelling a great deal. I have to read a lot to be informed about Youth Movements and pedagogical questions and in our spare time we like to walk in the wonderful surroundings. We also study Italian.

This is all for today. I hope to have answered your questions and am wishing you and your family all the best.

Yours,
Otto Frank

This was the first time Otto mentioned his wife, though not by name. Otto married Elfriede "Fritzi" Geiringer eight years after the war. He was introduced to her by Fritzi's daughter, Eva, as they were all traveling by train from the concentration camps back to Amsterdam. Fritzi had lost her husband and son in the camps. The mother and daughter had survived against insurmountable odds. And now, the young girl was excitedly pointing to the familiar man in the crowded train. "That's Mr. Frank! He's the father of my friend, Anne!" Eva and Anne had been playmates in the neighborhood, and Otto and Fritzi had never known each other until that point. Eva introduced the two, and in November 1953, Otto and Fritzi were married.

In careful, large script I answered "Mr. Frank"—I was still calling him that, for we were rather formal in our respect for each other in those early years. Also, I seemed to write to him as if in a foreign tongue—in very convoluted sentences, carefully screening out my young personality and presenting myself far more seriously than I remember myself to be. I do know I was older as a teenager than I am now.

A year later after a flurry of postcards to each other, I referred to his advice. I was still in high school.

My Dear Mr. Frank,

. . . In your last letter you might not recall this, but you answered my letter in which I asked your advice about my future as becoming an actress. Your opinion is one I shall remember and will greatly consider. You told me to join a drama group either in school or outside and not depend on becoming so much well famed as becoming a good person and raising a happy home.

Amen! Although my parents told me the same thing, somehow its just that third someone to get the point across completely and cause me to seriously take heed to what has been explained to me. I'm obnoxious, I know! Seriously, your advice was more than I could ask for and I thank you for taking the time to consider my plea in the midst of your own worries. I've joined drama class at my school, dearly love every minute of it and you were absolutely right! I was in a Shakespeare Festival at the University of California and the experience was one I shall never forget! I wish you and Mrs. Frank would have

seen the excellent acting that the kids my age displayed
—it was so exciting!

Before I end this letter I just wanted to ask how
your work with the German youths has been coming
along. Do you think that I could help by writing to
them giving them some insight of the American Jewish
teen ager? Or in that matter do you think that the
American teen agers could help in any way? If we could
help you in some way lift the curtain of prejudice and
ignorance that many of the young German people have
gained from lack of knowledge about the Jews or the Nazi
Regime, would it not be a great step in the sway of peace
without prejudice? I would love to hear your opinion.

I signed the letter "Always, Cara Weiss."

Mr. Frank answered this last part in a little note to me.

It will interest you to know that work at the Int.
Youth Center is progressing and groups of young people
from different countries are coming there to attend
conferences and to have discussions.

With kindest regards—very sincerely Yours,
Otto Frank

It was during this time that I starred in my high school
play, *Our Town,* as the character Emily—truly a high point of
my life. I'd fallen in love with George, the male lead character, played by Tony LaRocco, a worldly and beautiful boy
who I remember looking like George Chakiris in *West Side
Story.* And I also recall how he laughed at the fact that I didn't
know how to kiss. He was right, but I don't think he knew

how in love that Emily (a.k.a. Cara) was with George (Tony)! To this day I have Emily's last speech in my kitchen. And whenever I need to cry, I recite it out loud, convinced that I've just given an Oscar performance:

> . . . It goes so fast. We don't have time to look at one another. I didn't realize. So all that was going on and we never noticed. Take me back—up the hill—to my grave. But first: Wait! One more look. Good-by, good-by, world. Good-by, Grover's Corners . . . Mama and Papa. Good-by to clocks ticking . . . and Mama's sunflowers. And food and coffee. And new-ironed dresses and hot baths . . . and sleeping and waking up. Oh earth, you're too wonderful for anybody to realize you. Do any human beings ever realize life while they live it?—every, every minute?"
>
> —Emily, from *Our Town*, by Thornton Wilder

Anyway, I was teetering on the brink of leaving the nest, and I turned to Mr. Frank. He responded:

March 9, 1962

. . . I quite understand how you feel being seventeen years of age now. It is natural that on one side you want to be independent and on the other hand you are not yet enough sure of yourself so that you still need a certain support. I only wish that you continue to appreciate the love and care you found in your parents' home. It is one of the evils of American youth to try to show an outside independence and to overlook the real values of life. It seems to play a big role to have as many dates as possible and to be popular, neglecting a steady development of the character. . . . How nice that you enjoyed so much playing such an important role in Wilder's "Our Town." We have seen the play some time ago and liked it immensely.

In July of 1962 I wrote to Otto about two more "firsts" in my life.

My Dear Friend,

. . . My summer isn't terribly exciting I must admit—but it has proved to be quite *profitable*—I have a *job!* I'm working for a finance company. It's quite a wonderful feeling to be able to be somewhat independent of my family. It's a *secure* feeling—now *I* can lend my *parents* money! . . .

My braces on my bottom teeth are coming off before school starts much to my delight! Well, my mother always says, "If you want to be beautiful, you've got to suffer!" And that goes for those awful "metallic monsters" on the teeth, too! So much for growing up pains! Right now the phase of many young "scholars" of my age is to be *negative* and *critical* of the world. So many young men my age have desperately tried to convince me of the futility of our world—the stupidity of having religion—the frightening aspects and admirable aspects of *socialism*, *communism*, *liberalism*—and any other *ism* to be known! I listen to my dour faced "Clarence Darrows" and "Bertrand Russells" with closed ears. To quote an appropriate tune from the musical, "South Pacific"—"they can call me a cock-eyed optimist." I love *life*—maybe not *all* its aspects, but basic *Living*—I love!

I want to thank you for giving the Anne Frank Foundation my address—I shall keep in touch with them always. Anne is very much alive in my eyes and in millions of others—I hope to keep a part of her philosophy on Life instilled in my heart and soul forever.

With deepest respect and admiration I remain

Lovingly,
Cara Weiss

October, 1962

Dear Cara,

Thanks for your kind letter. I am glad that you feel more mature now that you have a job and that you earn money for yourself. This feeling might help you, but seems to me not to be the only reason. You have more experience in life—you are growing up, it is your own development.

You are right not to take the bragging of the boys about negativism too serious. It is a fashion and the age, that makes them doubt at all values—but they will grow out! Follow your own conscience and conviction and have a *positive* standpoint in life!

It will give you more satisfaction and firmness.
Kindest regards, also from my wife, and love

Yours, Otto Frank

In 1962–63 the political scene was a cauldron beginning to stew and boil over. Federal troops were sent to the University of Mississippi to force the school to enroll black James Meredith. Troops remained at the university until Meredith graduated in 1963. Here, one man had to fight for his dignity just to graduate—a black man in a white world. And I knew nothing of such pain or indignity facing my own graduation.

. . . I'm no longer "little"! I'm going to graduate high school this February and then I'll be a *college girl!* Can't believe it—just can't! I'm going to be eighteen soon and even *that* thought kind of shakes me up! So much for shocking realizations—

Jan. 21. 1963

Dear Cara,

. . . Just a few lines to thank you for your last letter and to wish you all the best for your exam. . . . I am glad that you feel more grown-up now and am anxious to know how you will like College life. You'll make new friends and get interested in many items.

Good luck and kindest regards

Yours,

Otto Frank

I was now attending Valley Junior College. My grades weren't good enough to go straight to a university, and frankly, the smallness of Valley's campus was a perfect way to ease me into mainstream university life. I was very happy.

2-28-63

My dear Mr. Frank—

I am now in college! I truly can't believe it—it has opened a whole new world to me. I've met the most fascinating, challenging people—and I suddenly am overwhelmed with a wonderful new sense of *freedom!* I love growing up—each new stage, each new day offers such excitement. I often feel as if I'm on the brink of something terribly mysterious or unusual. If this feeling accomplishes *anything* at *all*—it simply keeps me in an *optimistic* frame of mind! In college I am taking Anthropology, Psychology, Spanish, Theatre Arts and Modern Dance. My favorite is Psychology. I still disagree with a certain Dr. Freud though! Personally I think the man was mentally warped and *terribly* frustrated! The *nerve* of him making a simple dream into a complex, symbolic monster! His theories I could do without!

. . . People who know that I am corresponding with you constantly ask so many questions about you. I take such pride in enlightening them with such a small bit of knowledge of the dear gentleman I've so grown to love.

Last semester my high school put on the moving production of the story of your Anne. Mr. Frank, your *whole family, as well* as Anne will remain immortal in the hearts of the peoples of the world. What a warm glow you must have within you to realize that.

I hope this letter finds both you and Mrs. Frank in high spirits and good health.

I am enclosing my graduation picture for you.

With warmest thoughts and wishes—

Cara

April 2nd. 1963

Dear College Girl,

Thank you for your enthusiastic letter and the photo. I compared the latter with snapshots you sent me in former years, you certainly changed. Growing up is exciting—if you are aware of it. Not all young people are though! They just live without thinking really about it. I am glad you are feeling fine and happy in your studies even if you do not like the Freud theory.

. . . I was glad to hear that your High School performed the Diary and I hope that they succeeded in conveying to the audience something of Anne's spirit. Sometimes I have the impression, that it is played, as any other play—and forgotten.

I am going to Amsterdam nearly every month, it is difficult to build up an organization and I have a lot to do. At present we are preparing a pamphlet and as soon as it is ready I'll send it to you.

With all good wishes—as always yours

Otto Frank

It was 1963, the year of *To Kill a Mockingbird,* my most cherished movie of all—and the march for racial equality by two hundred thousand in Detroit. The waves of protests in Birmingham, Alabama, in April and May gained tremendous support for the civil rights movement. Police resorted to dogs and fire hoses to break up the demonstrations. It was horrifying to watch on the television. I couldn't believe it was real. I'd never seen people treated like that in my life. What was happening to the world?

It was during this time that I remember talking for hours to my father and telling him I thought I would convert to the Bahai faith. I was ready to join Martin Luther King in Alabama and march with him and his people. I just didn't understand how my temple and my people weren't more involved in the integration cause. It seemed that all the rabbi ever talked about was Israel. I felt so helpless and lost. In truth, most of the leaders involved in integration on all levels were Jews. I soon discovered this. Then the horror began escalating until the impossible happened. Medgar Evers, the field secretary for the NAACP, was shot and killed in June.

And on November 22, the worst nightmare of all— President John F. Kennedy was killed by Lee Harvey Oswald in Dallas. Could this be happening? I stood riveted under the campus loudspeaker as it announced the end of Camelot: "President Kennedy has been shot in an assassination attempt. . . ."

23.11.63

Dear Cara,

. . . We also were shocked deeply by the murder of Pres. Kennedy and we do feel this loss for the world. He was an extraordinary personality, whom we admired and loved . . .

Yours, Otto Frank

I sent Otto an edition of *The Family of Man*—a photo essay on the human condition throughout the world. He was both moved by the book and the emotions I expressed to him in the dedication.

February, 19, 1965.

Dear Cara,

 . . . As each one of us has had hardships and sorrows, we feel grateful to have found each other and though we shall never forget the past and our dear ones, we achieved to have a positive outlook on life. In this attitude it is a great support to have still family, especially my wife's daughter, her husband and their 3 little girls (living in England) and devoted friends. Besides there are the daily reactions to the Diary of Anne which show me that she has not lived in vain and the work connected with the Anne Frank Foundation, Amsterdam.

 . . . Thanks again and warmest regards to you and your dear ones in which my wife joins.

 Yours,

 Otto Frank

In those days, the Beatles were bigger than God it seemed. They stormed the music scene, leaving Beatlemania in their wake. The world had never seen or heard anything like them. Everybody's hair got longer as soon as those mop heads hit the States. The "flower child" look started around this time—blue jeans with T-shirts and long hair. Wire-framed glasses hit big. So did miniskirts and body painting, knee designs of painted or pasted butterflies instead of stockings, along with beads, feathers, and sandals.

I took up the guitar and was singing at "hootenannies"—a real folkie like my heroes, Judy Collins; Joan Baez; Buffy Sainte-Marie; Peter, Paul and Mary; Pete Seeger. The top radio hits then are still some of my favorites today: from those dazzling Brits, the Beatles' "Yesterday," Petula Clark's "Downtown," "Mrs. Brown, You've Got a Lovely Daughter" by Herman's Hermits, "Satisfaction" by the Rolling Stones, and back in the States, the Righteous Brothers' "You've Lost that Lovin' Feeling," and "I Got You, Babe" by Sonny and Cher.

I had graduated from Valley and was now attending UCLA. The following letter sounds like I was deliriously happy. I don't remember it that way at all. Strange.

February 2, 1965

. . . I am now living at UCLA—it is a tremendous university with around 25,000 students—I'm so *nothing* here—and yet I'm so happy! I'm 20 minutes from home—I talk to my family practically *every* day—we write—my parents try to come to the dormitory as often as possible—and *still* on my own! I entered a new world this February, Mr. Frank. I have met, and am constantly meeting new, stimulating, intelligent people. I have decided I *think* that I would like to teach dramatics in high school. I'm majoring in Theatre Arts and minoring in English. My classes are like electricity, they are so thrilling! Our room is adorable—my roommate, Rita, is an English major and we share many hours with talk about authors, poets, and that wonderful universal subject—Boys!

Not to digress from this prevailing subject in my life—I wanted to tell you that I saw you on the television program "Twentieth Century" and was very moved by your words. I saw you and heard you for the first time and so wanted to *really* speak with you. I admired the strength and conviction in your whole presentation. The point that you brought up about Anne expressing the fact that although she said that she believed that there was good in all people, she was still young and full of youthful naivete about life and people. She certainly must have realized that there existed some persons without any *true*, *deep* goodness from within. It is only now, at the age of 20, do I now put people off their pedestals and accept the world without the rose colored glasses. I find that what I see now, is maybe not as beautiful, but it is human and real and *Life*—not fairy-land.

I hope that your work and the ideals of Anne will, indeed unite the curious, knowledge-seeking youth of today—and leaders of tomorrow.

July 28, 1965

Dear Cara,

. . . I can imagine that your new life at the university changed your whole outlook and that your studies are most stimulating. You are very lucky that you have such a nice room-mate with whom you can exchange your views and also that, though you are now on your own, you can keep close contact with your family.

. . . Please tell your cousin and his friends that we are still remembering their visit with pleasure and we could understand very well that during their European trip they liked to look a little adventurous. We surely would not recognize them without beards.

As to my interview on TV I must tell you that I thought it was my duty to cooperate, though it was difficult for me to speak about the past. By the way I have been asked to write an article for Ladies' Home Journal about Anne, which I did. It probably will be published in fall.

✆ 3

Love and Marriage

Otto Frank was there for me when I changed college majors as fast as I changed socks. From dance to drama to English, my dear Basel "guidance counselor" was much more tolerant than my UCLA counselors. He was there when I contemplated the meaning of "greatness"—and the possibility of a mixed marriage. That was when I turned twenty-one . . .

February 2, 1966

I am now twenty one (as of New Year's Eve) and the chronological change hasn't really added any new dimensions to my character only a few extra worries maybe.

Being twenty one, regretfully hasn't altered my being, in the sophisticated, wordly sense that I had anticipated it to do. I now have only a year more of college and am *still* (surprised?) an English major and a Theatre Arts minor.

One of your letters to me that I most favor is the one in which you answer my question of "should I be an actress?" Your reply to me was one that I'll never forget: You said be a *part* of the theatre, but don't *become* the theatre, for it is impossible to raise a family and also be a successful actress. Through the years I've tried to reason out a way in which I could be close to the theatre and yet far away enough for me to retain my objectivity. I think that I've found my niche in life:

I want very much to write plays. I have had two scriptwriting courses in the university and I have been challenged and excited beyond words. My only setback is that I would never be satisfied with being *good*—because I love the sound and sight and touch and smell of— *greatness*. Does that sound idealistic or egotistical, Mr. Frank? What is your idea of greatness? Anne had that touch of greatness. What is it and how is it founded?

I hope to graduate from UCLA in a year and then I really don't want to teach but I do want to work near and around writers. Do you have any suggestions as to how I could go about finding such work? I've thought of working in New York or somewhere in Europe just to extend my little world and while I'm earning money, can learn more about people, too.

Another setback in my life is strangely the most beautiful happening: I am in love. Four of the most common words in an equally common sentence—and yet unique to me. I met him in a scriptwriting class this past semester and we got to know each other by doing a Tennessee Williams One Act scene together. I slapped his face and he threw me on the floor—and then I knew it was love! He aspires to be a television and/or movie director. I believe he can do anything that he wants to do.

. . . The setback in caring for him is the fact that he is not Jewish. He is a Presbyterian that believes in Adam and Eve and the miracles and revelations of the Bible.

He is not religious in the church-going sense, but he does *believe* more then he *dis*believes and that is what upsets me. Yet he knows very little about Judaism . . . he says his mind is open to learning about the Jews. He realizes that I could never raise my children in a belief other than Judaism—because it is so a part of me and my very existence. It is more a way of life—a philosophical retreat of the mind then is it a religion or a spiritual Nirvana offering prayer-promises like manna from the gods.

We both realized that you never appreciate something so much until you feel that you are going to lose it, and yet he says I musn't be pessimistic for through love and patience and maturity, there is a way. Mr. Frank do you think that I have reason to be negative—or do you feel that two similarly career and interest geared people can find the happiness that they claim can exist on mutual love? Do you know of any good books or articles that we can read to help us?

February 11, 1966

Dear Cara,

It is not so easy to answer your last, long and detailed letter. I appreciate very much that you are writing to me in such an open-hearted and confidential way. You think that you have not become more mature though you are now twenty-one, but my impression is that you developed gradually anyhow. You cannot notice a change from one day to the other.

Whereas you had not made up your mind last year in which direction your study should lead you, you see how much clearer that your interest for everything connected with theater is a lasting one. If you feel that you can achieve something in writing plays, you certainly did the right thing in following courses on this subject. Perhaps psychology would be usefull too. But in courses you only can learn the technical side. You will need a lot of experience in all sorts of human problems and relationships. So in leaving a job as secretary of a writer, or work in a publishing firm to become an editor or go into journalism, perhaps with the view to write play-critics.

If you really have the gift to become a good playwright, it will break through. Do not forget however that everyone with ambition is hoping for greatness—or at least success, which is not the same. Even if someone produces something great, it is frequently not recognized directly. But a real work of greatness survives generations.

Now to the great news that you are in love. I am so glad that you found a person with whom you have so much in common, whom you admire and who reciprocates your feelings. I am sure this love makes your life richer, but I fully understand your problem. My older brother married a non-Jewish girl. Both were not at all religious, but anyhow my sister-in-law offered to become Jewish, but my brother did not think it necessary, the more as they had no children. A year ago my nephew, who is an actor at the theater in Basel also married a gentile, a darling girl we all love very much. She had been an actress too, but gave up her career. They too are not religious and I am pretty sure that if they will get a child, it will not be baptized. In both cases the difference in religion and education did not influence in any way their life.

To my idea there is one most important question. If your friend is deeply believing in Jesus as son of GOD and the MESSIAH, I regard it as a great obstacle. This would always hurt your feelings and would create the greatest difficulties in the education of children. But if his belief is based more or less on the ethical principles of Christianism, then I do not see why you should not find a harmonious way of married life, as these principles are in fact based on the Jewish laws. Of course it needs much understanding from both sides anyhow. It surely would be good if you would get some books about progressive Judaism for your friend to read—from one of the many libraries of conservative or reform synagogues. . . .

5/15/66

My Dear Mr. Frank—

. . . Your letter in which you gave me such beautiful advice about mixed marriages and my career is a prize possession of mine. You gave me much deep thoughts to digest and dissect. It was certainly encouraging of you to relate the incidents of intermarriage in your own family. Marriage is still way up there on the pedestal. It is still intangible, unreal, and not foreseen in the near future. You have to know yourself and find security within your own self before you can ever hope to be a strength to a loved one. I haven't yet found that contentment.

I hope some day I can relax with myself, because when that day comes, I will be ready to accept the responsibility of marriage. Thank you so much, Mr. Frank, for your optimistic words on this topic. I don't know if I can yet accept such optimism.

I'm finding growing up, being a woman, beautiful and a little frightening. I'm not that sophisticated where I can't still find a good cry or a strong, warm shoulder, or a call from home, a great source of pleasure and comfort.

How I would love to talk to you! To see you, to walk around the streets and sights that are yours. There is so much yet that I've to learn from you, and there is so much yet that I have to ask of you. How do you maintain a constant degree of objectivity when all the world is groveling in cruelty, hypocrisy, selfishness? Do you stand up on a soap box and Billy Graham them, or do you role with the punch and hate yourself the rest of your life for having a backbone of jelly? Do you let your hair grow long, wear black tight boots and picket while all the little people turn their backs and complain how terrible the rest of the world is? I admit, I have a certain, growing desire to vent my anger, my thoughts.

Yes, I still want to be a writer, but I've decided not to associate with the showbiz writers, the fast talkers, smooth movers, synthetic aesthetes. They are a discouraging dime a dozen, and I've discovered by some disenchanting experiences that I want no part of them.

I've come to encounter many meaningful discoveries, epiphanies as Joyce's Stephen Dedalus in *Portrait of an Artist as a Young Man,* had so called his daily realizations. And one of them is my love for you. I feel that you are so a part of my life. I don't like to undress my thought waves to many people, so I have garbed them in letter form to you. And through the years you have closeted them and made me feel that you've believed in me. I can't thank you enough for sharing your thoughts, your philosophy with me. Anne knew in an annex what has taken me six years to grow to know about you. I feel very fortunate.

To just fill you in on newsy news I'll tell you the latest in these here parts. My roommate, Rita, graduated from college last week! It was a beautiful ceremony, and it gave me inspiration that should last me for a *least* another year when, glory of glories, I'll be set free! My sister, Laura, graduates high school tomorrow night! She is speaking at her graduation and practically is walking off with every honor conceivable! (It's times like this that I wonder if I was adopted . . .)

My parents, God bless them, are well and wonderful. They have kept us starving students fed with their surprise overabundance of groceries every time they come to visit us! Rita and I are still working at the Bank of America, and truly love it! The people are from all walks of life, from every status group and practically every nation and creed. It's actually just a miniature U.N.!

Our apartment is adorable: tiny, glowing, orange and turquoisy, filled with odd shaped bottles (I collect them), guitars, (we both play), albums (folk, classical, musicals, movie themes), here a collage with bright colored clippings and paraphenalia with a progressive, fringing on hostile poem (written by guess who), there books and magazines, more bottles (I said I loved them), some artistic photographs of children (taken by an artist friend of Rita's), a cupboard without a door, (the manager said that the cabinet-maker said that there would be a detainment of his services because of the war in Viet Nam—now really, that gullible we are not!), also a leaky faucet, a telephone that dials itself, (really, I was alone when it started to dial from the inside, and when it finished I was already begging forgiveness for being the devil's advocate—I thought for sure that the gods were going to get me this time!) and letters, cards and pictures. I wish you could see it. I wish I could see you!

8/19/66

Mr. Frank!

I've missed you so!! I hope that you and Mrs. Frank are well—*please* if you have a moment, scribble out a bit of a note to me. I must talk to you soon! Mr. Frank, you don't know how much I think of you and value our brief, newsy written thoughts across the miles. I've always cherished a constant dream of some day meeting you, but too much school and not enough money have kind of burst that bubble. Our letters have made the broken daydream a lovely alternative though so please *don't stop talking to me!!!*

. . . I'm feeling much more optimistic since our last talk, but then this is still today, and tomorrow is yet to come. . . . Knock on wood, spit three times and hold your breath—with God's help—I'll be graduating either in March or June of '67 and I *can't wait!* I aspire to go into advertising—it's a very hard, competitive field, but I'm keeping my fingers crossed that I can be hard and competitive right back! I'm still very much in love with Kent and hope with all my heart that *that* dream, of eternal life with him will some day come true. We have a lot against us—but even more for us. . . .

26th August 1966

Dear Cara,

. . . before we went to England we spent a week in Amsterdam where we attended the International Youth Conference at the Anne Frank House. It was most interesting and stimulating and young people from 9 different countries took part. I suppose you received the programme and I am sure you would have been very much interested in the theme "Is there a place for religion in the modern world." Most of the young people of different creeds were longing for something to believe in, but did in general not like the existing forms. But for me not only the lectures and discussions were important, but especially the personal contacts. After the conference I received . . . a letter from a Jewish girl from England who had met at the conference a young German boy. In getting to know him better she completely lost her prejudice against Germans.

. . . You wrote that you lost much of your idealism and that you are so sorry that the world is in such a mess and you ask me what my standpoint is in this respect. I know that a single person all by himself cannot bring about important changes, but nevertheless one should not be indifferent and everyone of us has the duty to do all in his power to help join the forces of peace and understanding. That is why I believe in the Anne Frank Foundation and work for it.

. . . I was glad to hear that your friendship with Ken gives you happiness though it involves many problems. Nevertheless it is surely right not to hasten developments and to have a long time of probation. . . .

11-5-66

Dear Mr. Frank—

. . . Your thoughts have a very soothing effect on me. My gentle German philosophic friend of *seven* years! Thank you for the strengthening effect you have on me as well.

I am now supposed to be studying for an exam, but with the beautiful music that is playing, and with the restlessness of my mind, my thoughts strayed to you. I hope to graduate from the university in June—I'm truly looking forward to that eventful day.

. . . I'm in love—and I am loved—so what *else* is there to feel?! The world still troubles me—but I've realized that I guess I kind of trouble the world too! After all, to my chagrin, I've discovered that *I'm a people, too!*

Kent and I are taking classes in Judaism every Tuesday evening and both love it! Thank you for your very valid advice in this matter. He doesn't realize that I've planned his reading material—(He'll be saying 'Shalom' in his sleep!). . . .

The backdrop of these benign meanderings was a gathering storm of fury. Vietnam was in full bloom. U.S. troops numbered 389,000 by the end of 1966. Huey Newton and Bobby Seale formed the revolutionary Black Panther party in Oakland, California. The Chicago race riots hit big—it took 4,200 National Guardsmen and 533 arrests to stop the madness. And for the first nine months of '67, a total of 164 riots broke out in major cities causing one hundred deaths and over two thousand injuries. "The Ballad of the Green Berets," by Sgt. Barry Sadler, was played over and over again. Blacks were already wearing their hair Afro-style. Whites were wearing the long, straight dos.

As I counted the months to graduation, I hummed along to Simon and Garfunkel's "Sounds of Silence," the Beatles' "Paperback Writer," "Penny Lane," "All You Need Is Love," the Doors' "Light My Fire," and the Rolling Stones' "Ruby Tuesday."

During that time, there was a write-up saying that Otto Frank would be going to Munich to a trial against war criminals.

I sent my friend a telegram:

2-4-67

Some times are harder than others to believe that people are really good at heart. My love to you in a very hard time.

February 6, 1967

Dear Cara,

I was very much surprised when I received your cable this morning and thoroughly moved by your thoughtfulness. It was so sweet of you to show me in this way how strongly you are feeling with me.

I am writing you immediately because I want to tell you that the papers were wrong writing that I would go to Munich personally. I never thought of doing so and was only represented by my lawyer. Of course I am following everything up in the papers which is rather exciting and besides I have to answer many questions of journalists who want to know my opinion. Some are ringing up from abroad even from Moscow. You surely are right that those accused cannot be regarded as normal human beings, they worked like computers without heart or feelings. But now at least two of them show signs repenting.

In all this lawsuit Anne is regarded as a symbol for all the unknown victims.

I hope you are well and happy and I suppose that you are very busy . . .

4-14-67

My Dear Mr. Frank—

I'm so sorry for not writing you sooner, but at the time you wrote me to reassure me that you didn't have to experience that trial investigation, I was in the midst of academic and internal chaos! I was so relieved to know that you didn't have to go through the past again—thank you for answering me so fast . . . it meant very much to me. Much has happened to me, dear, dear friend.

After *eight* years of written conversation—I've got, I do feel, the most wonderful news yet! Let me say *two* wonderful newses: #1—I graduated UCLA in March!!!! —no, I still can't believe it! *Me,* a college graduate! #2— the best news of all—and quite rightly, should take the precedence over news #1: Kent and I are going to be married *July 9th* of this year!

Yes, Mr. Frank—I'm engaged as of January 23rd—I have been in a cloud—a *frenetic* one at *that*—but still a joyous cloud! Kent proposed in an old-fashioned way— he surprised me with the question and the *ring*—just the way I had hoped and dreamed he would. He was never forced into the position—and so he felt freer to choose the right time and moment. It hasn't all been so easy, as you must already know, Mr. Frank. As I once told you before, my Kent is Presbyterian—a point that has made our relationship the talk of the temple and of our community. It has been harder on my father I think, than *any* of us since Dad works at our temple. People have talked about me as if I have done something *wrong*—even *indecent*. Rabbis have discouraged us— thrown horrible, frightening—utterly cruel statistics at us about the *odds against* our marriage ever succeeding— and we are having a time finding a Rabbi that has taken us under his wing and won't grant his approval to marry us until we have together read certain books on comparative religion—intermarriage—and Judaism. We have already attended a series of classes in Judaism last year and plan to continue this year—but since Kent won't convert—our marriage is not supposed "to work." I'm not bitter as I was at first—because everybody's reaction has, quite honestly, taken me by surprise.

I *wish* I could talk to you! There is so much that I have to learn—to ask you—to tell you. I love Kent. He loves me. We are not so naive that either of us truly believes that is what love and marriage is all about. Kent seriously wants this marriage to work as do *I!* He won't convert because he is emotionally tied to his religious background and now that I've learned more about it, I can see why. I visited his family in Missouri over Christmas, and we all fell madly in love with each other. Thank God both families are behind us—I don't know *what* we would do without their support! Don't you think it would be just as terrible—I must say much *worse*—if Kent converted only to please me and make things easier for *other* people? What kind of a Jew would he be then? Is *that* Judaism? I cannot convince myself of that. I'd rather he be sincere and remain as he is—then become a hypocrite in his subservience to the common consensus! He has made me happy—and for some *one*—beautiful person to continually do *that* to me—is the ultimate in accomplishments! He changes my temporary laughter into *continual* joy and he makes me almost, religiously chant Browning's memorable words, "Grow old along with me, the *best* is yet to be . . ." I have changed from a little girl to a woman with him and I think that now I can honestly say that there is nothing more in all the world, I'd rather be than his wife.

I'm not so naive to believe that we're different than others, Mr. Frank—but I do believe—mainly because of Kent's undying optimism, that if you want something badly *enough*—you sweat blood for it and block your ears to the roar of the negative "nays" and hear only the positive "yeas." Our children will be raised Jewish—with a mixture of two credos—some foundation only a little bit of Presbyterian pie with their matzoh ball soup! . . .

. . . I am working at Young & Rubicam, Inc.—an advertising agency as you know—as a copy secretary. I work for the copywriters—attend a class held by one of the writers every week—and *pray* that someday—*soon*—I'll be a copywriter! I *love* the field! It's challenging and electric and wildly imaginative! (I got the job in between my finals and my engagement!) Oh the greatest happening of all would be if you and Mrs. Frank could come to our wedding! I know it's not going to happen—but I can *dream* can't I?

May 27, 1967

Dear Cara,

. . . Now first of all I want to thank you for the two lovely photos marking two important events of your life. Though your graduation is the high-point of your studies and certainly a great achievement, your engagement means a lot more for your future life.

Looking at the photo of you and Kent, your radiant happiness reflects upon us and we are sending to both of you our heartiest congratulations.

I can imagine the big problems confronting you, but I know from all you have written how seriously both of you have thought about the question of the difference in religion. As you know I am very broadminded and I understand that none of you wants to convert. It is a great blessing that both parents agree to your marriage and are a support for you. Do not mind the disapproval of others. The main thing is that your personalities are well matched and you have respect for each other's conviction. I am very glad that you are in agreement about the very important point of the religious education of your children, as this is in many cases the base of difficulties.

I would be very interested to know the name of the Rabbi who showed so much understanding for your case. Of course we too would love to be present at your wedding, but you are right that this will not be possible. We wonder where you will settle down and we understand that this will depend on Kent's decision if he will continue his studies or accept a job.

You can imagine how excited we are about the situation in the Middle East. I am deeply worried and depressed to the agression of the Arab States behaviour of its so-called friends who do not take any action. For me Nasser is following the example of Hitler, both have openly propagated their plans and the world has not reacted until it was too late.

If Israel is not helped very soon and the solemn

promise of the Allies that the golf of Akaba will remain a free international water-way is not kept, then Nasser will go on with his intention to destroy Israel.

I am sorry that my letter is ending in such a gloomy way, but I know that you will understand my feelings. . . .

June 25th 1967

Dear Mr. and Mrs. Weiss,

My wife and I want to thank you very much for your kind invitation to be present at the wedding of your daughter Cara.

As you can imagine it is not possible for us to come to the U.S.A. for this occasion, though we would love to attend this happy event. You know that I have been in correspondence with Cara for many years and that I always took great interest in her personality and her development. My wife and I are sending you our best wishes.

Very sincerely yours,
Otto Frank

1-14-68

My dear Mr. Frank,

I had hoped to write you much sooner than this but just never got to it. I haven't stopped thinking about you now that I'm a married woman. Many is the time that I've been brimming over with so much feeling that I've wanted to share it with you.

. . . I've had this weekend to really reflect on these past six months (can you believe it?). Mr. Frank, you've known me for *nine* years. I grew from a young girl to a young woman in that time. I wrote you about my changes, my fears, my loves, my hates, and now as a young woman of 23 years—I write you and tell you that I have never in all my life—been happier. You always told me to be patient with life—to not run away to the theatre—to finish college—to be more tolerant of the world that angered me so (it still does—but I'm not overpowered by it all—the anger—*or* the world). You listened while I stood on my soap box—and you acted like a dear friend—a grandfather. And now after all that emotion of growing up—I *thank* you, dear, dear Mr. Frank—for being *there*. I want you to know of my *happiness* now.

Kent is an electric, alive, dearly sensitive human being. . . . It's funny how *more* religious the two of us have become in trying to combine and analyze our philosophical and religious beliefs. We hope that by the time we have children, God willing, we will be strong enough in our differences and similarities to cope with any problems our children may face. (They will be raised Jewish—but we see no reason for Kent to have to convert just to make it easier for everybody else.) We've combined our prayers into a beautiful Friday night ritual. We light the candles, say the Kiddush and the Lord's prayer—and our own spontaneous one. We feel so glowy and good afterwards.

Before our Rabbi would consent to marry us, since Kent wasn't converting, he talked many hours with the both of us and had us read some wonderful, thought-provoking books, the best being *Jews, God and History* by Max Dimont. Kent really got a lot out of it. The Rabbi is a young, brilliant highly moral individual. He wanted to feel right about us. He didn't want to be burdened with a heavy conscience—to feel that he was doing a wrong thing for *us* and for *him* by marrying us. Only after he talked with us and my parents and felt that Kent was indeed a religious person—attuned to the Jewish ideals and way of thinking but emotionally a Christian—after he saw that Kent couldn't convert to Judaism just to be a Jew in name only—he agreed to marry us.

I love Judaism and Kent has grown to know it—to respect it—to feel comfortable and confident that his philosophy would not be lost in a Jewish home. I've learned and grown from Kent, and I guess I really don't want him to be anything but what he is. I'm not all confused or unhappy like I feared I would be. We had a Christmas tree and a menorah for the holidays. (I don't think Santa Claus will be in our home, however. What about *Moses* coming down the chimney?—no . . . I think that little legend will just do better *outside* our home!)

I meant to tell you that Rabbi Maller surprised us and quoted a passage from *The Prophet* at our wedding—the passage on "Marriage." It's our favorite book and passage from it and we couldn't believe our ears when he came forth with that *beautiful* excerpt!

My job is getting more challenging only because the writers are giving me a chance to try my wings. I hope to have a portfolio of samples by the end of six months and by then, the Copy Supervisor said he'd help me find a writing job if they didn't have any openings at Y & R! I really am looking forward to that time!

3-68

Dear Cara and Kent,

At the occasion of your first wedding anniversary, my wife and I are sending you best wishes. We are happy, that you are happy.

Warmest regards and love,

Yours,
Otto Frank

March 26, 1968

Dear Cara,

Time flies and though I wanted to answer your dear letter sooner, I just did not find the leisure. When I read your heartwarming reminiscences about our relationship since so many years and how you are valuing it, I was really moved. Now I want to tell you that the confidence you always had in me was a precious gift from your side. Having contributed a little to your develop-ment, gives me satisfaction. . . . I was extremely glad to hear that you and Kent are so happy together . . .

. . . I have great respect for your Rabbi who was so broad-minded to respect Ken's religious feelings not insisting on his conversion. Though you both adhere to your own religions, you manage to celebrate holidays meaningful.

Now about us. We had a wonderful winter-vacation in the mountains together with the children and grand-children from England, who are always a great joy for us. This did us a lot of good and we stayed in good shape during the winter. I am still very active, going to Amster-dam nearly every month and working regularly daily on my correspondence together with my wife. In spring and summer we are expecting a lot of visitors from abroad.

In May however we shall be in London for some time and in July we are going to attend the Int. Youth Conference in Amsterdam as every year. The theme this time will be "Youth and Human Rights." In case you know some students or other young people who are going to Europe and may be interested to attend, it would be nice to draw their attention to it.

You know that the aim of the Foundation is to further understanding and to work for peace; though the state of world affairs is very discouraging, we must not give up. Anyhow we are very worried about the situation in Vietnam, for which we do not see any solution and about the tension between black and white in your country. We are following up everything very closely and we are very sad about the decrease of prestige and economical power of the United States. This influences also, we are sorry to say, the position of Israel, as America is not able to back it sufficiently.

We only hope that another president will be elected who will be able to turn things to the better. . . .

✥ 4

Political and Social Awakening

THE YEAR WAS 1968—etched in my mind. I can't ever forget it. Otis Redding was "Sittin' on the Dock of the Bay" . . . while we hummed along to "Hey Jude" by the Beatles . . . and "I Heard It Through the Grapevine" by Marvin Gaye . . . and then the world stopped. On April 4 in Memphis, Martin Luther King was killed by James Earl Ray. And on June 5 in the Ambassador Hotel in Los Angeles, Bobby Kennedy was killed in front of the world by Sirhan Sirhan. The young senator had just won the California Democratic presidential primary.

June 6, 1968

Dear Mr. Frank—

"America! America! God Shed His Light on Thee!" Today, Mr. Frank, I don't know whether I can ever sing that song and still believe in those words. I don't want to turn my back on the land I've loved so fiercely, but the foundation, the "free" soil beneath my feet is shaken. I'm frightened. And angry. And ashamed. And terribly lost in the poisonous atmosphere of fear . . . and hate. Bobby Kennedy is dead. Martin Luther King is dead. John F. Kennedy is dead. Medger Evers is dead. All shot by the bullets of mad men. Mad men who all some time in their sad lives cried out to their neighbors for help . . . and no one heard . . . or cared. Lonely men with scapegoats to vent their sick self-hate upon.

Bobby Kennedy. A saint? No. A Christ? No. No. No. A *Man*. A man with youth and anger. A quick-silver mind and body. A man not afraid of the mud or the darkness or the complexity of the ghetto or the slick city. A man that Charles Evers, the brother of the slain Medger Evers, believed in. The only white man he really trusted. And his feelings were echoed by the majority of the black people. Bobby Kennedy. A father and a husband and a brother and a son and the only hope for peace in the minds of millions all over the world.

Yes, the gentle, wise Senator Eugene McCarthy is a man I can believe in as well. Robert Kennedy wanted to unite with this man. He believed that together, their philosophies and their followers would bring peace to our broken nation, to our broken world. Where do I go now, Mr. Frank? Must I love and believe in my world with the paranoid distrust and defense mechanism that involves no real commitment? To play it safe and not love . . . because then I'll not be crushed. But then I won't have lived totally . . . wholely . . . will I? When your world was destroyed . . . how did you go about repairing it? How can I help strengthen the world that is falling around me? I can't cradle my crying nation to my breast and nurse it back to health. But I want to. I can't storm the U.N. and shake each man by his shoulders and beg him to *tear down the walls*. But I want to. I can't stand in the middle of our land and scream for everyone to turn and touch his neighbor's face . . . white hands on black cheek bones and vice-versa . . . see the loneliness in each other's eyes . . . hear the whisper before the scream . . . and the gunshot. But I want to. Will we ever see into each other's eyes? The beautiful American Indians . . . stony-faced and quiet in the silence of their neglected, unjust worlds. And the Mexican-Americans . . . their vibrancy stifled by crowded quarters . . . away from the big cities.

How can I bring a child into this world? What can I promise him? Freedom? Peace? Love? Tolerance? Tomorrow? I don't mean to be embittered. Or reject the substance, the core of living that these great men died for in their fight for peace. Bobby Kennedy is gone. And he was so briefly here. Just beginning to convince us of a peaceful tomorrow.

And I was just beginning to break down my defenses. To extend my hand to him. To be vulnerable in my love and respect for him. Tuesday I voted for him. As did the majority of people here, because he won the primary race in California. And then a mad man decided he was too great to contain any longer. And he killed RFK.

Thank God Kent and I have each other during this mentally and emotionally trying ordeal. We want to be strong. We don't want to give up and forget what Bobby awakened within us. Kent has helped me. When I start to strike out and hate the hate, he reminds me of the power of love.

You are a forgiving man. A man of strength and inner battle scars. I could use some of your morale plasma right now. I would like to help you, Mr. Frank, in the way you've helped me. I would like to write a pamphlet or essay extending the philosophy and love of Anne Frank. Your foundation is a beginning. A great attempt to reach the youth of the world and give them hope. Today's youth needs hope.

They need to believe in tomorrow. A beautiful tomorrow. A peaceful tomorrow. Not enough people know about your foundation. Let me help you awaken their knowledge of you and your work. Do you want this of me?

I feel a little better now, as do I always, once I've "talked" to you. And as you also know, I love you. Please tell me what is the date of your birth. I know it was some time in May, but you never let me know. I promise I won't embarrass you with a huge Cecil B. DeMille production. I just want to know. Since I'm already late, I wish you much health and happiness and a happy, happy birthday and many, many more!!!!

Please, Mr. Frank, don't think I'm rejecting my America. I love my country. My people. I just feel so helpless now. At this moment, I can't see any shedding light. I feel so empty. Along with your prayers, Mr. Frank, please include America.

Thank you for listening, dear friend. God Bless You.

Much love, Cara

June 19, 1968

Dear Cara,

Your last letter written under the impression of the shock you felt after the assassination of Robert Kennedy moved me very much. It was not a letter—it was an outcry. I understood you so well as I share in many respects your feelings. I too, as well as millions in the whole world are mourning over the death of R. Kennedy and those who before him became victims of fanatics. They all were excellent men on whom the hope of many good-willing people was set upon. If the murderers acted out of personal grievances, one could not blame "America" for these crimes, But one cannot help to be suspicious that powerful, evil groups are working behind the screens. If this is really the case and they can extend their power and succeed in eliminating the progressive forces, I see the future of America very gloomily.

If nothing will be done to end the Vietnam war and to help the poor and neglected masses, there really is the danger of an uprising, a civil war. The pathetic words of Rev. Abernathy addressing the crowds at the march of the poor, that this is the last chance of a peaceful solution, makes one shudder.

But there is still an alternative. There are millions who are feeling their responsibilities just as you do.

In your democratic system there is the possibility of influencing affairs by election. Much will depend on the next President and his advisers. As far as we can judge from here however, not one of the candidates can replace Kennedy. Though McCarthy has about the same aims, he seems not to have the brilliant, energetic personality, but one must hope that he will grow with his duties, should he be elected. Or should the republican party be given a chance with Rockefeller?

Though the situation is far from satisfactory, you must not [be] desperate. Never give up!

I remember to have once read a sentence: "If the end of the world would be imminent, I still would plant a tree today." When we lived in the secret annexe we had the device "Fac et spera" which means: "Work and hope." I do not know, if I ever wrote this to you.

So you should not ask if you should bring a child into this world. Life goes on and perhaps your child will bring the world one step further. Anne who died as a victim of injustice and hatred, achieved something for mankind in her short life. Perhaps the new generation will live under quite different circumstances than we can imagine now and will have a quite different feeling of happiness.

You are right that at certain periods of my existence the world around me collapsed. When most of the people of my country, Germany, turned into hordes of nationalistic, cruel antisemitic criminals, I had to face the consequences and though this did hurt me deeply I realized that Germany was not the world and I left forever.

When I returned from concentration camp alone, I saw that a tragedy of unexpressible extent had hit the Jews, my people, and I was spared as one of them to testify, *one* of those who had lost his dear ones.

It was not in my nature to sit down and mourn.

I had good people around me and Anne's Diary helped me a great deal to gain again a positive outlook on life. I hoped by publishing it to help many people in the same way and this turned out to be true.

When later the Anne Frank Foundation was established I wanted it to work in the spirit of Anne's ideals for peace and understanding among peoples.

But as you can imagine we are working on a rather small scale as we only can reach and try to influence people who are coming to the Anne Frank House. It was always my wish to make it the center of an international organisation with branches in many countries, which would have to deal with their specific problems. Up to now this was not possible.

You are asking me what you could do to spread the hope which is contained in Anne's Diary to the benefit of the youth of your country. Maybe that through a pamphlet, as you propose it, an action could be started and an Anne Frank group formed. This group should issue a paper in which young people could express themselves freely, trying to find positive answers to the many-fold problems which divide America.

U.S.A. has the sad reputation to have the highest rate of crime and dope in the world. Why not fight against the horror and crime films and literature? I know that big business would oppose the oppression of such films. Ammunition and war-material industries are against the limiting of the sale of weapons. Only youth with ideals could take a stand against these evils. This is just one idea.

But how could such a paper be financed and

distributed? I am thinking of subscription and many voluntary helpers.

I am so glad that you have Kent at your side in these difficult times. He gives you strength and comfort. The harmony between you should enable you to cope with every situation. I hope that the opportunities he got by winning a scholarship will prove to be fruitful for him.

Please excuse my English. Of course I could express my thoughts better in my own language.

Let me thank you for your good wishes for my birthday. It was on May 12th.

Write again if you feel like it. My wife and I are sending our love to you and Kent.

Yours,
Otto Frank

8/27/68

Dear Mr. Frank:

Without sounding too gushy, I have to say that you're wonderful. Your letter in answer to mine after Robert Kennedy's death meant more than I can begin to express. You gave me encouragement. A little of your philosophy. You gave me inspiration to plant that tree today . . . even when my strongest intuition tells me there will be no tomorrow.

What would I do without you, dear friend? My Kent found strength from your letter, too. He thinks so much of you. And what a wonderful surprise to have you remember our anniversary! You and Mrs. Frank are beautiful people! We couldn't believe a whole year had passed already. And we still like each other. Amazing!

As anniversary gifts to each other, we exchanged albums that we made for one another. I made an album of all the little mementoes and pictures collected from our courtship days, and Kent made one of our whole first year. Kent's really great. He's so artistic and such a perfectionist! I wish you could see them. The house reeked of glue for days after our massive projects, but the end result payed off. Two sentimental nuts.

The world situation is still as miserable as it was yesterday and the day before. The situation in Czeckoslovakia is very depressing. I pray that those strong people won't give up their fight for freedom . . . no matter what. I had such hope in their success. And our up and coming elections are a farce. I've never seen or heard or felt such confusion in my life. Can you imagine people actually taking Nixon and Maddox and Wallace *seriously*? It's frightening. People (and I don't mean to deny my claim to peopleness) never cease to amaze me. They hear and see only what they want to. Fear blinds and deafens them. They all want to do "the right thing" and they think by closing their doors and windows to the world they're doing just that.

Kent and I are going to join the American Civil Liberties Union dedicated to aiding minorities or impoverished peoples. It's very powerful out here and from what we've heard from talking to some very fine people, very successful as well. Our white America also has to be elevated. There have been a series of documentaries each week on Black America. They have been brilliant and very moving as well as shocking. I'm ashamed of my ignorance after being enlightened of the extensive subtle cruelty and degradation done to the black man in America. I'm tired of shaking my head in disbelief. I've got to do something. Now.

I wonder, and this is what I've been meaning to ask you. Do the majority of temples in America know about the foundation? When I asked a woman who is in charge of the Jewish youth organization at U.C.L.A. called Hillel, if she knew about the foundation, she didn't know anything about it and wondered if you have any kind of plan to awaken these youth organizations as well as temples and churches of the foundation and the summer conferences. She was very enthusiastic about it and said she would help in any way she could. Do you want me to compile some sort of general list of these organizations, write a standard letter of introduction and then you could include all the information you wanted to about the foundation? Please let me know. I want to help you.

What I would love more than anything in the world, is to meet *you*. Just the other day I told Kent that I would love to write a book—a bibliography about you. Kent said that the only way I could really do that would be if I met you. And I said I know. I think that people should know you. You owe society the secret of your wondrous philosophy of life. I'm sure you have been asked this of you before. But this is just one of my Number One dreams. If we could work some way out of interviewing via tapes . . . but then I wouldn't see your expression . . . the way you held your hands . . . turned your head. . . .

Well, from the state that this letter is in, you'd never know I'm an executive secretary. (Not for long I

hope. Last week I started going on interviews at different advertising agencies. I'm looking for a writing
position.)

I don't mention this in my letters to Otto, but during
this time I journeyed to San Francisco with my friend Nancy
Vaughan, carrying tons of deli food, blankets, and high hopes
of joining forces with the Native Americans on Alcatraz
Island. What I'd hope to accomplish I'm not quite sure—and
neither were they. Always a "Walter Mitty" dreamer, I think I
saw myself as some kind of super-writer who would tell the
world of the Indians' plight and save them all and then they
would embrace me as their honorary Indian-in-residence. In
truth, I met up with a ragtag group of tribal parties—having a
party. They were not at all overjoyed with my presence and
didn't think I looked one iota like an Indian, as Nancy asked
them. "A blue-eyed Indian, no way!" Buffy Sainte-Marie was
nowhere to be seen. And not even one painted pony. My life
has followed a pattern of disappointing scenarios like this. If I
would just "Let It Be," as the Beatles sang . . .

September 27, 1968

Dear Cara,

In your last letter you mentioned that you are
looking for a new, more creative job and I hope that you
will find one which will give you more satisfaction and in
which you can use your wonderful gift of expressing
yourself in writing. It is always a pleasure for me to read
your letters which show your whole lovable personality.
Just as you would like to meet me, my wife and I would
love to meet both of you. From our long correspondence you could perhaps make out that I do not like to

be in the public eye and therefore it would be embarrassing for me if a book about me would be written. So please do not follow up this idea.

As to your suggestions about the Anne Frank Foundation, there are two aspects: one is to make it more widely known so that young people would visit the house when travelling in Europe to meet young people from other countries there and to attend our International Summer Conference. It is not possible to propagate the Foundation and its aims from Amsterdam, so we should have a center in U.S.A. helping us in this respect. Our survey of activities for 1967 has just been published in Holland and is now being translated into English. As soon as it will be ready, I shall send you one and perhaps you think it worth while to send extracts of it to Temples and Church-groups.

Then the Foundation badly needs financial help, as I have written you before. We are trying to make the Foundation tax exempt for U.S.A. knowing that substantial amounts will only be given if people can deduct them from their taxes. In principle I never wanted to ask Jewish organisations for financial help as I think their actions should be concentrated on Israel. As soon as we get a decision about our application I shall let you know.

Just as you we are deeply worried about the world situation. By the invasion of C.S.S.R. Russia has shown its true face and making use of the weakness of U.S.A. and the disagreement of Europe is trying to extend its power. So the elections in your country affect all of *us* here in Europe and are of great importance in view of the situation in the Middle East. Whereas the Russians are backing the Arab States openly all the time America does not dare to do the same for Israel. So we only can hope that a new war can be prevented. One feels so powerless in the game of the supernations. . . .

As to us we had a pleasant holiday at the Belgian coast with two of the grandchildren from England. Later we went to London and I attended a conference of the World Congress of Faith where representatives of many religions took part. It will interest you to hear that there was also an all faith service. . . .

In honor of my birthday that year, Otto Frank did the most incredible thing. He sent me a note that said this on it: "2 Trees in Israel in the name of Mrs. Cara Wilson for her birthday. Planted by Mr. O. Frank, Birsfelden."

May 21, 1969

Dear Mr. Frank:

. . . Your beautiful birthday gift to me moved me very much. Thank you, thank you! I can't help feeling that it was a living symbol of your words to me one time. When you said that even if you feel there will be no tomorrow, you must plant a tree today. I often think of those words and I feel that those two trees are Kent and me. Someday, with God's help, we'll plant a tree . . . even if we fear there won't be a tomorrow. Maybe someday we'll visit my gift. Or better yet: the *doner*.

. . . I finally got a writing job! I'm writing this letter in the lovely confines of my own office, with my own plant, telephone, desk, chair, window, walls, curtains and typewriter! I'm a beginning copywriter at Chiat/Day Advertising Agency. It's a small, up-and-coming agency in L.A. and out of six writers, I'm the only woman writer. I'm really having fun. The accounts I'm working on aren't what you'd call the most creatively stimulating subjects (computers, welding company, a modern piece of equipment for moving boats and things!), but it's a start. And you never can tell when an interesting tidbit like how to move boats might affect my life. Well, I mustn't complain. I'm told beginning writers can't be choosy. . . .

I have to get off the soap box quickly. As you know, once I'm on it all the anger wells to the surface and you have to wade through it 'till the end! You might know about our vicious race for mayor. A sick, demented, wildly paranoid present mayor: Yorty vs. a fine, liberal man: Bradley who won't play Yorty's name-calling/slandering games. Bradley just might possibly be California's first black mayor. If not . . . oh lordy. I won't be what you'd call a study in restraint! I won't talk about noxious Nixon. I won't talk about the sickness in conservative thinking. The thinking that is not so slowly sweeping our land. The thinking that fears sex education and communism and atheism and integration. I won't talk about these things. My blood pressure, you know.

I will say that life has been good to me. Aside from the constant anger that adds fuel to my thinking/creating, I'm happy. I'm only frustrated that there's only one me. A very little me compared to all I'd like to do to make things better.

In 1970, I was eating yogurt—the latest health craze—and buying only "organic" or "natural" foods, free of chemical fertilizers and pesticides. Funny, I never liked yogurt. It was just high on the "should" list. (Do we ever really like those "shoulds" in our life?) The look was unisex and "hot pants"—those sexy short shorts that you wore with platform shoes and a cute little cloche hat. I did all of that. False eyelashes, too. I was also playing the guitar all the time. I considered being a singer/songwriter for about a blink. One song during those days has since become my own personal mantra—one that even talked to me in a prophetic dream: The Beatles' "Let It Be." . . .

That was the year when the Beatles disbanded, and the Chicago Seven caused such havoc. Jerry Rubin, Abbie Hoffman, Rennie Davis—the whole bunch of them were in the news for their rowdy, antiestablishment, antiwar antics during the 1968 Democratic National Convention. David Dellinger tried to hold a courtroom reading of the names of Vietnam war dead. Once Rubin and Hoffman wore judicial robes during their trial. They passed out jellybeans. They screamed furious epithets at Judge Julius Hoffman. It was wild. Meanwhile, Vietnam was raging. Even though President Nixon announced his intention to withdraw additional 150,000 troops by the year's end, heavy U.S. bombing continued targeting North Vietnam in retaliation for their attacks on our reconnaissance flights.

By now Americans were made aware of a gruesome event—the My Lai massacre in March of '68. Over two hundred Vietnamese villagers were brutally killed by U.S. troops. Students and "peaceniks" all over the country were holding rallies to stop the war in Vietnam. I joined in and sang along as we held candles and cried, "All we are saying, is give peace a chance." And then, on our own soil, we had our own massacre. Kent State . . .

5/5/70

Dear Mr. Frank:

. . . Much has happened since our last talk. I am now working as a copywriter at a small agency near our home. For a while I was working at home for some small accounts. I got restless being so much alone and now am feeling more productive, more alive.

We hope that it won't be too long before we can buy a home to make room for some animals, plants, and hopefully *babies*. I can't say when that will happen, but just between you and me I don't think it's going to be that far away!

. . . We're both taking [guitar] lessons and find it such a wonderful outlet when things get too trying. Kent is crazy about it and is really great at it. If it weren't for those guitars, many times we'd give in to the depression that seems to permeate our country. I don't have to reiturate what these sad, sick, violent events are—you know about them. The most recent tragedy is the death of four students killed on a campus in Ohio—shot in peaceful action. They were protesting an immoral war. The troops that were called in to stop the rally were young men—scared by flying rocks and scared by a situation they had no right stirring up. They shouldn't have had guns in their hands. Guns at an anti-war demonstration. Doesn't make sense, does it? There's so much sickness going on here, Mr. Frank. It's very hard to believe in planting trees today—who knows if there will be air for them to live in tomorrow? It's not the kind of world I would choose to raise a child in. But, I'm also selfish. If my life isn't going to be long, I don't want to die without experiencing the birth and raising of a child.

Please forgive my pessimism, Mr. Frank, I don't mean to bombard you with these angry thoughts. I'm not giving up. I plan to use my writing as a weapon. There are organizations blooming around town that believe in pure air and peace and they need help selling these "products," both Kent and I plan to assist them. At least we'd feel we were doing *something!*

I wrote the following flier for the Anne Frank Foundation in May 1970:

"What can we, young people, do to prevent such horrors and to create a liveable world?" These words were repeated over and over again in the diary of a now very famous young woman. Anne Frank. Today, they are echoed by the young in loud and impassioned voices. In a day of hostile gaps separating generations and races and religions, there is a place where everybody can get it together. The Anne Frank Foundation. Established May 3, 1957, in Amsterdam, the Foundation is a meeting place for young minds to mix and grow. It has welcomed visiting individuals and groups from all over the world. It is not just for Jews. It is for peoples of all religions. And political views. And they come in all colors. Visiting professors, doctors, scientists, politicians and artists direct classes throughout the year. The classes center around current topics. They are fresh and challenging and many times painful. They are beautiful.

The Anne Frank Foundation has survived because of a father's belief in a daughter's belief. Mr. Otto Frank lives in Basel, Switzerland, and spends all his time furthering the growth of the Foundation. He believes that the future of the world stands in the faith of the young: "Even if you feel there is no tomorrow—you must plant a tree today."

The Anne Frank Foundation is a beautiful tree.

And it is there for young people to climb. No matter how old they are. For more information on how you can attend or contribute to the Foundation, please write to: The Anne Frank Foundation, Prinsengracht 263, Amsterdam.

June 29, 1970

Dear Cara,

. . . We were glad to hear that you and Kent are satisfied with your work and that you are happy together.

It would be wonderful if you could carry out your plan to come to Europe next summer and that we could meet after having been in contact with you for so many years.

Recently we had the visit of several young American friends and they all were very unhappy about the situation in U.S.A. not only about the war in Indochina, but also about the tendency to facism not only in the administration but also in a great part of the population. This really is frightening and a growing recession may stimulate this movement. We have been told that everyone opposing this trend is regarded as a communist. It is difficult to think of America as a free country any longer. Anyhow I just cannot imagine that there are not enough people who are realizing the danger and it is more important than ever that the positive forces join so that perhaps in the next election a change to the better can be brought about. Let us hope that in the meantime Israel will not become the victims of the bad and shortsighted American politics. . . .

August 6, 1970

Dear Cara,

   . . . We are all longing for peace and justice and just now there is a little spark of hope that settlement may be reached in the Middle East.

My tree of hope began to blossom. But not everyone's world was as beautiful as mine during that time. The Black Panthers—whom I had supported so passionately—were now becoming increasingly more violent. Their furious confrontations with the police were becoming widespread, and Panther party leaders Fred Hampton and Mark Clark were killed in a dramatic Chicago police raid. And while I was shaking my fist in outrage, I was also patting my tummy. . . .

℘ 5

New Life

September 16, 1970

Dear Mr. Frank:

Fantastic news! We're going to be parents! Kent and I are really excited by it all. I found out officially last week. The doctor confirmed my queasy stomach and said that there was a reason for it: I was around two months pregnant. I wish I could say that you and Mrs. Frank are the first to know, but I've been so thrilled about the news that I tell anybody and everybody I know and don't know. Everybody, that is, except where I work. We really can't afford my quitting at this stage, and I just hope I can hold off from saying anything for awhile. At least until nature starts showing off.

Meanwhile, on top of everything, we just bought a beautiful old house in the hills. Its got a world of trees and plants in abundance around it, lots of wood and stairs and something I've always wanted: an attic. There's quite enough room for you and Mrs. Frank when you come to visit us. So, we refuse to allow you to say no. We're planning on that day. And we're stubborn, you can't convince us otherwise. You've *got* to come and stay with us! It's the kind of house I know you'd love. We're painting it now. Tearing down things and building more. Kent's been working hard. This is our first house. Our first baby. We're very lucky and very happy. When I think of all the traumas I've gone through growing up. I've written each stage, each peak of emotion, each aching age of recognition—maturity to you, dear friend.

I've never felt so good about people as do I now. My anger with them still sharpens my focus, but I find that I have more room for love than I ever did. Yes, the news does seem to get worse, but in subtle, gentler ways the people seem to get better. I am contradicting myself. I defended the Black Panthers. I stood behind Angela Davis. I believed in the rightful anger of the militant. And then they showed up backing the Arabs. I felt like shaking them. Screaming at them. They have judged the small, selfish ghetto Jew, the liquor store owner in Harlem, the grocery store merchant in Watts, the little man who has conned them and thrown them aside— they have judged this sad representation of a people and put all Jews in his category. They have overlooked all the hippie and yippie leaders—mostly Jews—who have fought along side them. Who have raised their fists— their white, Jewish fists—high in the air next to the black fists. I think that the Black Panthers could do so much for their people and consequently for our country. Their anger could be used so beautifully. It could raise black egos out of their dusty graves—out of the ghettos—into leadership. The blacks could lead white, silent majority, chalky, frightened America into greatness. They could kill ignorance with the fire of their beautiful soul. But the Panthers make it very hard. They prefer personal power. And the death of human flesh, rather than the blood of stupidity. I shake inside with anger and disappointment for them. And yet I love them still. Maybe my love will get to them some way or another. I'm not giving up. Little Israel never will. American people are slowly realizing that. The courage of that tiny country is giving us courage. I've got a lot to overcome. And we *shall* overcome. By God, we shall. I'm finding that in the pain of our existence, people are becoming closer together. Sensitivity groups are popping up everywhere. Nude marathons are taking place. People want to touch each other. See the primitive, animal, pureness in each other. They reach out. Organized religions aren't filling this aching gap. They are too removed, too obscure, too alienated from the world, from the next handclasp. Religions with stucco walls are dying. Pure spiritual religion, the original religion of the rebellious Moses, the forgiving Christ, the questioning Confucious, is emerging. People are holding hands for the first time. This is what excites me. Challenges me. Gives me some hope for my future child. This is the tree I know will be growing tomorrow. The tree of love. It was conceived with it. I pray it will grow tall with it—even after I'm gone.

October 15, 1970

Dear Cara,

What wonderful news your last letter brought us! From every line of it we can see how happy you are that you and Ken will have a baby.

Without having known that you are pregnant you bought the beautiful house in the hills in which your child will grow up. This must be more than sheer coincidence. We are wishing from the bottom of our heart that the future life of the Wilson family in their new home will be a happy one and though there will be ups and downs, we are sure that your mutual love will overcome everything.

There is only one thing we regret—that we shall not be able to have you with us here next summer, because you will not come to Europe as you had intended. Though you invited us so cordially there is no chance that we shall come to the States. Believe me I would love to be with you and Ken after we have been in correspondence for more than 11 years, following every phase of your development, but you forget that I have grown older too and am now 81. Though I am in good condition, I need a lot of rest and a visit to America where I have a geat number of good friends would be too great a strain for me.

So I am afraid we shall have to wait until the three of you can come over. There are so many young American couples who visit Europe with small children.

We can imagine that you and Ken have a lot of work repairing and painting the old house and shaping it according to your taste. But you surely love to do as much as possible yourselves as then it becomes more a part of you.

You are writing that your whole outlook on life has changed somewhat since you know that you will be a mother. You see hopeful signs in developments and we agree that it is good if young people are taking an active part in trying to abolish injustices and all sorts of grievances. but we cannot follow your views regarding the Black Panthers. Not only because they are backing the Arabs, disregarding the true facts, but also because the leaders incite the whole movement to violence not for the good cause, but to get power. If they really would get it, they would misuse it and discriminate others. To my opinion problems cannot be solved by terrorism and violence . . .

November 17, 1970

Dear Mr. Frank:

Thank you for the lovely letter. It was so good hearing from you and Mrs. Frank. But don't write us off completely! We still plan on seeing you both as soon as possible. As soon as the baby appears and our first year house worries disappear, we'll know where we stand financially. And I hope it's close to you two. We're counting on it.

I am enclosing a confirmation service that will take place at my parents' temple. My father wanted to make sure you saw it, he thought you'd be pleased. The graduating youth from the temple will read the words of your Anne. It's a beautiful tribute to her and to their futures. If you feel like it—if you have the time, you might want to either tape some sort of introduction to be heard at the evening, or a letter from you would be read at the congregation. If you don't want to, that's fine. Dad just wanted you to know about this evening. He's putting it together and is very excited about it . . .

November 28, 1970

Dear Cara,

Thank you very much for your kind letter and the text for a confirmation service, which as I suppose, has been held in Canada several years ago and which will be adapted by your dear father for a confirmation service in his congregation.

I was highly moved in reading it as Anne's words form such an important part of the service and I hope that the young people will be inspired by her message and that her faith, courage and optimism will be meaningful for their future lives.

Forgive me if I do not send a special address, but everything I could say is already contained in the text of the service.

I am sure that this confirmation-service will be a big event for your father's congregation and a memorable day for the youngsters and their families.

We were glad to hear that your plans to visit us have only been postponed, but not given up. We hope you are feeling well and are sending you and Kent our love. . . .

While we were singing "Joy to the World," Three Dog Night's big hit, South Vietnamese troops invaded Laos. How far away that awful war was to me, in 1971. In contrast, my world was filled with such happiness. We had this soulful black-and-white-pawed lab named Buffy (after Buffy Sainte-Marie, of course), whom we considered to be our first child. She was the light of our life. But then new life entered our home in the hills: On April 27 in the early evening, after seventeen hours of hard back labor and every Lamaze trick in the bag—from rolling pins to baseballs—Kent and I welcomed our beautiful Robert Ethan Wilson. We drove precious Ethan home to the sound of Tin Tin's "Toast and Marmalade for Tea."

October 9, 1971

Dear Cara,

Since the announcement of the birth of your baby-boy we did not hear from you.

We did write to you at the time, sending our congratulations, and also sent a music box for the little one. We do not know if it ever arrived.

In July I gave your address to a nephew of mine who visited Los Angeles. He tried to ring you up, but could not reach you. We are worried. . . .

10/16/71

Dear Ones:

Never was I more disappointed by a letter! We never received your music box. I've called the post office and will do some more sleuthing throughout the week to try and locate it, but I'm afraid it got lost in the mail. We're just sick! I wish I could say something appropriate like, oh, it's the thought that counts. And it is. But, I'm *still* fuming! Of course you would be wondering why the silence after sending us such a beautiful gift. On top of your gift being lost, we've changed our phone number to an unlisted one. So when your nephew called, he got some more silence. That made me more furious. How I would have loved to have him over. . . .

Of course, I could have still written sooner, true, but my life has been totally wrapped around the entire being of one little Ethan. He is a fantastic child. Yes, I am echoing the words every mother says about her child, but I choose to forget that. He is fantastic. And he looks exactly like Kent!

I wish I could say that there's a lot of me in him, but, aside for a quick mannerism or two, he is the spitting image of his Dad. Huge blue eyes and tremendous dimples on both cheeks, a little one on his chin. He's all arms and legs (Kent is 6′2″ and we are both lanky)—a very big boy who, at six months, is already keeping me going non-stop all day. He's beginning to crawl, to sit, he grabs and reaches for everything, spits and blows loud, determined bubbles, flashes a radiant grin or a serious, unblinking stare at you, laughs a lot, is impossible to diaper: the minute he's put on his back, he flips over on his stomach and tries to crawl away. He loves our dog, Buffy, and the dog loves him. They kiss each other, stare at each other a lot. I could go on and on, but I'll save you from my gushing. I'm in love. He's got the kind of wild, enthusiastic spirit that Kent and I hoped he'd have. Just six months on the earth and he's already a fire of a personality.

I think I told you that we were going to have him the Lamaze method, or a studied form of natural childbirth. Well, we did it. Which makes this little boy even more special to us. Kent was at my side throughout my labor. We had trained six weeks for that day. Panting and blowing through our rehearsed labor. Now I was panting and wheezing and blowing for real. And Kent never left my side. He rubbed my back with a rolling pin. Fed me ice chips. Timed the contractions. Talked non-stop in my ear. Never let me concentrate on my pain, but made me focus on my breathing the way we were trained and that's how Ethan came into this world. He saw both of us seeing him.

We screamed when the doctor said, "It's a boy!" Oh, how we wanted a boy. I had tried to convince myself that I would in no way be disappointed if it was a girl. But I knew I was lying to myself. And when I saw that he had Kent's dimples, I knew God had really gone overboard this time. He made us very, very happy!

I am still nursing Ethan, which is such a pure wonderful way to get to know your baby. He's eating lots of solid foods as well, but the nursing won't stop until he let's me know he's ready. (No, I won't let that carry on too much longer. I mean, he might not be really ready until he's eighteen, but that dedicated a mother I'm not!) I feel like Earth Mother every time I hold him to my breast.

Never have I felt so calm and peaceful as when I am nursing. Kent says he never knew me to have such patience. And it's true. I'm the most *im*patient person with everything and everybody except Ethan. Anyway, he better enjoy it while he's a baby. Because I know this won't be true once he's old enough to fight his own battles. We are having some pictures developed and will send them to you soon.

Life has been very good to us. Although with a new house and new furniture, lots of paint, repairs, carpeting, etc., etc., etc. we're finding that our budget is a bit tight. We still plan on seeing you people someday very soon as soon as we can relax financially here. We're not giving up on our very special plan: to meet you and talk to you and take hundreds of pictures and give you lots of hugs and kisses. It's just going to happen!

Just to keep you up to date. As I said before, Kent has been very busy—his work required lots of travel. Most of the time he's producing and directing his commercials three at a time. It's the kind of work that involves him every moment. It's hectic and demanding and frustrating but, once it's going well, it's beautiful. Each big commercial is like a little movie. And it's the kind of pace and challenge that Kent loves . . . I've found it just a little hard to adjust to the pace he's in. Some days I find it harder than others. Especially since I haven't had much luck getting any freelance writing. . . . This has been my main frustration.

I am so sorry your gift never arrived but Kent and Ethan and I thank you with all our hearts for such a lovely remembrance. We still received your note after Ethan's birth and that really was enough. I hope this is a good and healthy year for you both. I realize that I forgot to wish you a happy birthday, Mr. Frank, so please consider yourself hugged and kissed now. Thank you again. Much love . . .

November 20, 1971

Dear Cara,

We were so glad to hear from you and I would have answered right away to your lovely letter if I had felt well. But this was not the case lately and I could not attend to my correspondence for some time. Now I am alright again.

We are sorry that our little present did not reach you and so we bought another music-box which we sent air-mail registered. We hope Ethan will like it.

Time flies and now your little darling is already 6 months old. We understand fully your enthusiasm about him. No wonder that he has already now such a strong personality having you and Ken as parents. We are looking forward to receive snapshots of him.

You are describing everything from his birth on so vividly that we have the feeling to be his grand-grand parents.

Nowadays not many mothers are nursing as long as you are doing it, but it is certainly good for the baby and I can tell you that my wife's daughter was nursing her children for 8 months.

There is only one thing however which struck us: that you are allowing Buffy to lick the baby. It is nice that he likes the little one so much, but it is unhealthy.

You are writing that little Ethan is keeping you busy all the time. But as soon as he will start walking, he will need still more attention. So we believe that during the next year you will not be able to do much creative writing. But as you have an urge for writing we are sure that later on you will find the time to do so.

It will be of interest to both of you to hear that Peter Nero composed a musical work using as text passages of Anne's Diary. Now Jerome Schnur wants to take this work as a base for a TV production and negotiations for it are pending. We listened to a tape of the Nero work and we were impressed by it, as we think it could have a great impact on to-days' youth. . . .

We hope so much that you will be able to realize your plans to come and see us in not too far a future. After we have been in correspondence now for 12 years it's high time that we meet personally, and make the acquaintance of Kent and little Ethan. . . .

What a year 1972 was! That was when I saw one of my all-time favorite movies, *Harold and Maude*, to the tune of Cat Stevens's incredible sound track. We were all talking about *The Godfather* and Brando's powerful performance. I remember singing along to Don McLean's "American Pie" and daydreaming to Roberta Flack's exquisite "The First Time Ever I Saw Your Face," and of course, Helen Reddy's "I Am Woman." Well timed since the Equal Rights Amendment prohibiting sex discrimination passed the U.S. Congress. But it failed to win ratification by the 1982 deadline! The year also marked the beginning of Nixon's downfall. The Watergate scandal reared its ugly head.

This was the year Japan regained control of the island of Okinawa from the United States, and also when Nixon made his historic visit to China. Vietnam was as bloody as ever. Nixon ordered mining of Haiphong and other North Vietnamese ports. But by the year's end, U.S. troops in Vietnam only numbered twenty-four thousand.

I remember my imagination spinning when we sent the *Pioneer 10* space probe out into the universe with a plaque attached to it attempting to communicate with intelligent life beyond our solar system. Oh how I prayed we'd hear something. . . .

In the midst of all of this drama, my world was jammed with brewers' yeast and vegetable textured meat substitutes. Tofu was coming out of my ears, and even though I hated it, and hate it still, carob was my flavor of the year. It was one of those god-awful "shoulds" that I felt I should have. Yuck.

I worshiped health maven Adelle Davis and was consumed with buying and preparing only the healthiest, purest (and I'm afraid my family remembers it all as the yuckiest!) foods on the planet. I was happily involved in a playgroup—a bunch of Lamaze graduate moms and their babies Ethan's age. It was the "neighborhood" none of us had.

1/10/72

Dear Mr. and Mrs. Frank:

We received your bright red, round and adorable ladybug musical toy! What a fantastic toy! We are not kidding when we tell you that it is a real, true favorite with Ethan. He loves it. He chews on it, licks it, dangles it above him, and of course, sits in fascination when we pull the string and let it sing to him. It's a guaranteer to stop him from crying. And we *all* thank you for that!

Hope your holiday with your family was as fun as it always is for you. And especially wish you a happy, healthy New Year.

We just got back from spending the holidays with Kent's family in Jackson, Missouri. It's always a great deal of fun and, of course, it was more so this year because of Ethan. He was in the spotlight the whole time and loved it. He's a real ham—loves to force a real phony laugh when everyone's laughing around him. Does so many tricks now, it's hard to keep up with him! He "dances," crawls onto, into, over and around everything. He stands. Makes fascinating noises that feel so good on his lips. Spits. Pulls Buffy's tail, grabs the bones away from her; gets into her water bowl; pulls the floor lamps down onto the floor; flushes the toilet; grabs eye glasses off of faces, puts his whole fist into your mouth; doesn't like to sleep. Does play and laugh and go for hours. Lord, he's just eight months! That's Ethan. Two huge dimples on his cheeks. And complete mischief in his tremendous, blue eyes. Needless to say, he's got us and everyone else entirely wrapped around his little finger. He loves everyone. Smiles at complete strangers wherever we take him. Holds out his hands for you and the rest of the world to hold him. And still he's aggressive. Thought you'd appreciate the fact that now he pushes Buffy's face away when the playful dog tries to kiss him. He must have read your letter. He's a joyous child. I know all parents say and feel this way (or I *hope* they do!) about their own children. But he has made our lives so complete. So rich.

You don't know how close we got to possibly seeing you both this Christmas. True. Kent was going to shoot a commercial in Paris and Munich. He said he wouldn't believe the fact that we might meet! And then it fell through. They're going to shoot the commercial out here instead. I had mixed reactions. I wanted so much to see you. But then it would mean leaving Ethan behind with the family—I would have to stop nursing him. And honestly, I just wasn't ready yet. Ethan probably could take the weaning better than I could. (He's already drinking out of a cup as well as a bottle, as well as a breast. Variety is the spice of life.) Anyway, Fate kept us a family—now maybe Fate will create that opportunity again.

Please send some pictures of you two. I am sending some of ours to you. Thank you again, dear ones. Much love . . .

P.S. Exciting news about the Peter Nero musical about Anne. How's it going? More news please!

March 17, 1972

Dear Cara,

Thank you so much for your nice, enthusiastic letter. The photos of Ethan you sent us, are lovely and his looks fit your description. The more we look at them, the more we are caught by his friendly smile and the mischievous look in his eyes. If he was standing already with eight months he must be a strong and active child. We can imagine that the little boy is the center of the whole family.

Watching the progress of a child of this age, is a continuous joy for the parents. It is discovering every day a little more of its world and the experiences it is making and the impressions it is getting are important for the development of its personality.

We were very excited to hear that you nearly had the chance to come to Europe and to visit us. But as it should have been around Xmas time, it would have been very difficult to meet, as we passed our holidays in a winter resort where we stayed from December 20— January 6. So we are hoping for another occasion in not too far a future.

You ask about the Peter Nero project. After the contracts had been signed with him and the TV producer we had no further news and probably they are working on the script and the music. They got 18 months time to decide about the final production. I cannot interfere and just have to wait.

Here everything is fine. After a mild winter spring is in the air and in our garden the daffodils and tulips are already coming out. It is fun to work in the garden.

In February we have been in London for a week to visit the family there. Next week I am going to Amsterdam again. We also had many visitors from abroad and at easter-time we are expecting friends from Holland.

Keep well. We are sending our love to the three of you.

Yours affectionately . . .

I sent Otto the book *Jonathan Livingston Seagull* for his birthday. . . .

June 29, 1972

Dear Cara,

We were very pleased to hear from you again. Thank you very much for your good wishes for my birthday and the delightful book sent as a birthday-present from the 3 of you. We enjoyed reading it immensely and you are right that re-reading it gives one more and more insight in its philosophy. The bird's strife for perfection and self-fulfilment is described beautifully. It shows that it affords a strong character to live as an individual following one's own ideas. It is fascinating to read how Jonathan after having reached the climax of his capacities, learns that he has the duty to spread his message to his brethren. There is much oriental wisdom in the book. . . .

It was the end of 1972 and I was very pregnant with my second child. . . .

Dear Friends:

Here is another holiday and one we hope is filled with much joy, family and healthy, ebullient spirits. We are thinking of you both so much! We want to share a new joy with you. Going to have another baby this April! Very excited—I'm now six months pregnant and bigger than ever. We'd planned to have our babies this close—I know this year and next will be hassled, frazzled and diaper deluged but, we are still excited in spite of what everybody is warning us! (After all, what can we do about it anyway!)

Ethan doesn't know a thing about any such shared spotlight. He's a terribly funny, joyously active, curious 19 months old. He never walks—he runs. He imitates every sound—questions every sight—mimicks the world like a trained circus chimp. He has us laughing all the time. Makes a sound like a lion—a fire engine—a kitty, dog, frog, truck, airplane, etc.—wiggles his nose like a rabbit, puts a hat on and his false glasses and dances around in circles to some great tune in his head. We take hikes and walks together—join a group of other mothers and babies twice a week and let the wee ones climb, slide, squeal and romp all morning together. He keeps us going!

We wish and pray that we could be together—sitting around our fireplace and talking until the wee hours of the morning. We also want you to know, dears, that once we can work our finances out, we sincerely plan to make some sort of constant contribution to the Anne Frank Foundation. . . .

December 12, 1972

Dear Cara and Ken,

We were delighted to receive your sweet letter and the lovely photos you sent us. The one of both of you must have been taken at a very happy moment at a picknick enjoying being together outdoors and sharing your hobby. There is such a loving look in Cara's eyes, and the hart carved in the tree is a symbol of your harmony.

Your description of Ethan's character and behavior and the funny expression of his face on the snapshot complete each other. We can imagine him as an actor in a play written by his mother and directed by his father!

He must be a great joy to both of you. That he will get a little brother or sister soon, will surely be a surprise for him.

Our opinion is that 2 years difference between children is quite right. Our two older grand-daughters are also only two years apart. Of course we agree that it will be a lot of work and a mother has to give up a lot of her own interests for some time to devote herself entirely to the upbringing of the children. But this time also offers many compensations.

Thank you very much for the very special mobile you sent us. It is standing on the table of our living-room and it gives us pleasure to look at it and to think of you. For so many years we are hoping to meet each other, but with the new baby coming this spring, we certainly will have to wait another year or two. Let us hope that we stay in good health (we mean the two of us re. our age).

Your continued interest in the Foundation gives me great satisfaction and I am sending you by ordinary mail the report 1971 to give you an idea of the work done there.

For the coming holidays we intend to go to the mountains together with our dear ones from England. Wishing the 3 of you a specially happy 1973 we are sending you lots of love. . . .

In 1973–74, I was wearing headbands, pukka-shell neck-laces, and American Indian anything. Tattoos were a rage, though I never did that. Feminists were at their zenith, and the play-group women and I had some intense discussions over "I am woman/I am mother" conflicts. I was deeply into earth-motherdom and felt that the children were being lost in this passionate race of the sexes. *Roe* v. *Wade* shook the nation, invalidating state laws against abortion for women up to six months pregnant. Paul Anka's "You're Having My Baby" nearly caused a feminist war. Though staunchly pro-abortion, I had to admit I thought the song was lovely. I think they sent out a hit *woman* to snuff me out.

The movies then were extreme in every way—from *Last Tango in Paris* to *American Graffiti*. Pea soup would never be the same after *The Exorcist* made its debut. I loved anything Jim Croce sang, and John Denver's "Sunshine On My Shoulder" still "makes me happy."

The Vietnam War was coming to an end. The cease-fire agreement finally went into effect, and the last U.S. troops were withdrawn from Vietnam. By the end of 1974, the last U.S. prisoners of war were released. The U.S. government granted amnesty to those who evaded the draft during those Vietnam years. Unfortunately, for the returning vets, hell only continued—or got worse.

President Ford pardoned Nixon for the Watergate crimes. And on Yom Kippur—the holiest of Jewish holidays—the Arabs attacked Israel. The Six Day War. It was a bloody, horrible tragedy that rocked the world.

Yet, in 1973 something wonderful also happened: my beautiful son Jesse Kent was born. Amazingly, the same song, "Toast and Marmalade for Tea" by Tin Tin, played on the radio once again as we brought our second son home from the hospital. I was joyful.

August 25, 1973

We received your fantastic cradle gym! Thank you again and again! It's not only beautiful to look at, but it's Jesse's favorite thing to play with! Honestly—it's true—that baby grabs at it, talks to it, screeches in delight as it moves and rattles above his head. It's a delightful as well as a stimulating toy and we love you for thinking of our baby so creatively.

To keep you up-to-date on our roly-poly baby, Jesse: he's a big, cuddly, yummy child. We adore him. He's always smiling and cooing. He's terrifically strong. Already turns over and over—like to have you stand him on your lap—sits up so straight looking at everything that moves—giggles and chuckles at tickles and funny faces. He's so big that people can never believe he's just barely 4 months old. He's 18 pounds—27 inches long!

Wearing Ethan's clothes that Ethan wore at one year!

We take him everywhere—going places that his big, two-year-old brother goes: the park, playgroup, children's concerts, camping, he's so adaptable and peaceful. The noise level around our house is phenomenal what with two dogs and a roaring Ethan yelling out his existence for all to hear.

Jesse copes with us—he balances our life with his gentle, kissable spirit. Ethan has been so wonderful with the baby we can't believe how smooth the transition has been—we were worried things would be rockier around here than it is. True, things are crazy. Not a moment of time or quiet to myself. I look away for a minute and Ethan has the garden hose and he's watering our front-room rug—or into the refrigerator breaking eggs all over the dogs—or throwing dog bones down the toilet—things aren't exactly calm around here . . . But he seems to really like his fat, little brother. He's everyday gaining a sense of possessiveness for him—wanting us to be sure to take "Jassee" with us when we go driving—smiling at and kissing the baby even when he thinks we're not looking (which is more sincere!) and generally reacting in ways that make us feel he's not all together as shook up about the new little person in our lives as we so anticipated.

Kent is happy with a new job—a new direction in his career . . . Me—I'm enjoying this frenetic life. Of course I am loving every minute of once again nursing a baby—it feels so good having a cuddly, cooing infant in my arms again. (I don't know if I told you but after having a wonderful pregnancy—I had an incredible, fabulous birth experience. Just six hours of labor with

Kent by my side throughout as he was with Ethan, I was able to push Jesse out without any medication and no forceps—Jesse started coming out so fast that he was almost born without the doctor catching him! But he came back just in time and then placed our huge infant in my arms and let the baby suckle my breast on the table just minutes after his birth. A very moving experience for Kent and me . . .)

Each day seems to get a little smoother as I learn easier ways to handle two active, demanding little guys. And then I got some freelance writing that could be a sort of sporadically steady job and would help to balance out my life even more.

We think of you people often—wishing so much that you could meet and hold and play with our boys. You have been so much a part of our lives—my distant, dear adopted grandparents. Wish that we could be together now . . . What with the insane state of affairs in the world—at least the American part of it—is in, we find that we have to look for happiness, search for good reasons to be on this choking, festering planet. We have to find hope for our children to build on in spite of the rising economy, morbid violence, ecological wastelands, Watergate mentality . . . I just keep buying more plants to fill the house, take walks in the sunshine and groove in the smiles and laughter of my family. And then everything seems like we just might make it after all. Thank you dear ones for sharing in our happiness—we hope that you are both healthy and happy and that this year will be a full one for you. . . .

December 7, 1973

Dear Cara,

We were just planning to write to you at the occasion of the approaching holiday-season, when this morning we were surprised by your parcel at breakfast-time. We wondered what it would contain, as you are always sending us something special. We like "the butterfly on the rock" very much, as it brings in these gloomy winter-days the promise of a new summer to come. Thanks a lot.

We still have to tell you how much we liked the snap-shots you sent us some time ago. You and Ken look so happy and well having little Ethan at your side with his cunning look. One can imagine him doing all the mischief you are describing so humorously. You must have good nerves to take it this way. On the other picture on which you are licking ice-cream you look like a beautiful Gypsy. And baby Jesse is really marvelous, smiling already when he was only one month old. He seems really to be an especially well developed child and far ahead of his age. It is really a blessing that Ethan is not jealous on his little brother and a good sign of his character. As they are so near in age the 2 boys will soon be able to play together.

We were glad to hear that Ken likes his new job and that you have the prospect to do some freelance writing. You surely have a great talent for writing which shows itself in every one of your letters. . . .

Shortly ago we went to Mannheim, Germany

where our nephew lives with his family. He is an actor and we saw him in several plays among other is "Championship-season" which was also a big success in New York. The corruption it is showing is very depressing, as one knows it really exists.

As you can imagine we were highly shocked about the unexpected attack of the Arabs on Israel on Yom Kippur and are now mourning with all those who lost members of their families. Israel totally isolated can only count on the help of the United States which realizes the danger of the Russian imperialism in the Middle-East and so Israel is not only fighting for its existence but also for the freedom of the Western World. Europe however does not think further and is only concerned with the oil-crises. . . .

A small parcel is on the way to you containing a little something with pressed flowers from Israel.

Wishing you, Ken and the boys a wonderful holiday-season and a happy, healthy and successful 1974, we are sending you all lots of love. . . .

Dearest friends:

We received your beautiful flower-pressed coasters and we simply oohed and aahed over each fragile one. They are lovely and we thank you so much. Especially since the flowers were from Israel.

Our brother-in-law, Eli, was called back to Israel to help fight during this last war. We were so frightened for him since we knew he was involved in some highly secretive and dangerous work being that he was part of a specialized troop there. Thank God, he's back home now—greatly saddened since so many of his troops—his friends since childhood—were killed. A political war—with the world's oil dangling over the lives of a tiny nation. Israel fights on but I wonder how long they'll be able to do it . . . Russia is doing everything it can to smother the little country. But, I didn't intend to start out on a sad note, this is 1974 now and let's pray it will be a more peaceful year than last year was.

It always takes me days to get myself going again after the flurry of the holidays. I love the holidays so much! We went back home again to Kent's family in Missouri. It was an enchanting time with snow and sledding and a visit to an old farm and lots of happy, laughing children and adults surrounding us. Ethan had a fantastic time and we hardly saw him the whole time there. He was racing around with cousins from morning 'till night. He's blossoming into such a tall, wondrous person. Two-and-a-half and constantly talking, repeating and miming everybody's mannerisms—putting on a different hat everyday—waking us up wearing a cowboy hat, chewing bubble gum, wearing Kent's huge gloves and my sun glasses. At six in the morning! He has us laughing all the time.

And Jesse! That fat little guy. Almost nine months already and he's tremendous and doing everything he can to keep up with his roaring big brother. He grins and laughs all the time. Climbs up and almost down the stairs. Stands up to anything he can lean on. Flushes the toilet. Spills the dog bowl over and over everyday. Eats dirt out of the plants. Pulls our hair—and the dog's fur—and loves to be danced around the room and kissed constantly under his twelve chins. He's a joy and we're both finding our little guys sooo much fun as they grow into their own, distinct personalities.

I do find that there are days I wish I could just close the door and keep walking. But I've surrounded my world with many warm, intelligent women whose hands and heads are as full of children as mine and we find great strength in knowing that we're not alone and that our demanding little tykes will, indeed, grow up some day!

I'm involved in a mothering-child observation class with Jesse that has given us all such peace and direction—taught by a beautiful Hungarian lady, Madge Gerber, she has influenced my mothering-methods greatly. So I am busy. Still doing some freelance writing whenever it comes in and am doing more writing on my own now as well as resuming dance lessons. I'm much easier to live with when I've had some time to myself! And Kent is ever so busy. He's doing some of the most beautiful work he's ever done and enjoying new directing freedom. I'm terribly proud of him. We had so much fun together this holiday I just hate it when he has to go back to work—but that's reality and I never was good in dealing with it!

'74

My dearest friends:

It has been so long since we've had a good old talk. At least, it's been awhile since I've sat down and answered your lovely, newsy letter.

Enclosed in this package is a very much belated birthday gift for you, Mr. Frank—please send us a picture of you wearing it! Happy, Happy Birthday to you (and if you'd come out here, we'd celebrate it with much flourish—balloons, cake and ice cream and many kisses)—can you reveal your age? Also included are the most recent pictures of the boys, we thought you'd enjoy them.

Well, dears, life is spinning and more full each day. New school for Ethan—he is becoming more verbal and joyous everyday—running around here with a cape or pith helmet, cowboy boots or Indian headdress and the rest of him always stark naked. He sings constantly, mimes and more and more is capable of playing by himself or his new friends. He is growing into a person that I find more entrancing everyday.

And Jesse is Mr. Peaceful—whereas Ethan is an extremist, Jesse is like a beautiful young redwood tree—strong and resilient and someone who gives me a great sense of calm. He is also quite funny. There is something very silly in a more subtle way with Jesse. He is 15 months old—Ethan is three years old. Jesse repeats almost every word we say to him—he cries and laughs, waves, snaps his fingers, claps his hands, pretends to talk on the phone all on cue. He follows Ethan everywhere— eating anything Ethan hands him: plants, dog food, yogurt, books and paper—Jesse will manage to stuff it all in his always open mouth if Ethan gives his approval. We are joyous in the fact that they, indeed, love each other. They stroke each other's faces and play together constantly—as well as pop each other in the nose! We find life a real trip with these two! Kent and I are happy and well—knock wood—Kent busier than ever directing commercials and me chasing and rarely catching these crazies that greet our day every 6 AM—I also started teaching a movement class to a group of mothers once a week and still write sporadically. Alls well, dear ones, we love you both!

June 7, 1974

Dear Cara,

It is a long time ago since we received your last letter. We had intended to answer it much quicker, but it never came to it somehow. . . .

. . . In April we spent 3 weeks in Israel. By the way we did not know that you have a brother-in-law who is Israeli. As it was our 4th visit to the country we did not do much sight-seeing. Our purpose was to see relatives and friends and to show our solidarity with the people still suffering from the consequences of the Yom-Kippur war. Luckily there were again many tourists, among them numerous Christian groups.

In the meantime the political situation looks a little brighter thanks to the infatigable efforts of your German-Jewish Kissinger. Let us hope that he will give his good services also during the forthcoming negotiations in Geneva.

. . . We always have great pleasure in reading your letters, as you are describing everything so vividly and humorously. You are certainly a born writer and we are glad that you still find time to do some free-lance writing.

We can imagine that you and Ken are observing the growing up of your 2 little boys and are comparing everything Jesse is doing with what Ethan did at the same age. You surely can already judge a difference in their personalities.

It is wonderful that Ken is so satisfied with the work he is doing, but we understand that you are missing him when he is too much absorbed by it.

September 10, 1974

Dear Cara,

It is quite some time since we received your parcel and your last, charming letter. It was so thoughtful of you to send me something for my birthday, even belated. You do not seem to realize that I am an old chap, now 85 years old. As much as I like the T shirt I really can not wear it at my age, but I thank you for your good intention.

We were very pleased with the snap-shots of your 2 boys. They look so healthy, happy and lovely. You are describing their behavior so precisely that we can see them before us.

Ethan seems to have inherited his vitality from you, and though we do not know Kent we imagine that he is a calmer type and Jesse is taking after him. "Opposite characters are attracting each other" is an old German proverb. This is the case with you and Kent and also with the boys. They must be a permanent joy for both of you.

We can understand that you are reluctant to come to Europe as long as the kids are so young. After all you are writing they have a wonderful free life in your lovely old house and garden. It would be too difficult to keep them quiet in a hotel. As much as we would like to meet you all, we have to be patient.

✪ 6

A Visit Missed, a Visit Planned—At Last!

In 1975–77, I was garbed in peasant-style dresses and skirts (as I still am!). Seemed a natural look for me. Maybe my Hungarian roots surfacing. The "ethnic" or "layered" look, it was called. I wore baggy everything. Funky hats, boots, headbands. Later, I'd wear ties and vests—very Annie Hall-ish. And jeans, jeans, everywhere jeans. My favorite uniform even today.

The biggest deals were skateboarding and that hot dance craze, disco. The Bee Gees were synonomous with that popular move and sound. Their "Jive Talkin'" was a biggie, along with Elton John's "Philadelphia Freedom" and Paul McCartney and Wings' "Silly Love Songs" and "Listen to What the Man Said."

The last Americans were evacuated from Vietnam, South Vietnam surrendered to the Communists, and the Middle East battled on, while the movie industry pumped out some cinematic greats: *The Man Who Would Be King, Nashville* (how I swooned over Keith Carradine singing "I'm Easy"), *One Flew Over the Cuckoo's Nest, Jaws, Annie Hall, Close Encounters of the Third Kind,* and *Star Wars.*

Meanwhile, I was heavy into my family, two play groups, the L.A. Zoo, and a parent newsletter. . . .

My dearest friends—

    I walked into a book store—bumped against a book rack—heard a small thump! and when I looked down, saw what fell at my ankles: *Anne Frank: A Portrait In Courage*, by Ernst Schnabel. I bought it immediately, chilled by the strangeness of it all—why *that* book out of the hundreds that filled that store should fall at my feet?! I haven't read it yet, but felt deeply compelled, once again, to talk to my distant "grandparents"—every once in a while this great longing to be with you both—to talk about Anne—to know more about that great young woman with the Herculean faith in the good and the just of life.

    Please send me the most recent information on what the Anne Frank Foundation is doing. I would like to feel even somewhat part of it. I have been keeping a journal of both boys since their births—it has given me great joy to record these unfolding, little people—and I feel a sense of immortality about them, too. Somehow you don't completely die when you've left your thoughts behind you. Anne still gives me strength as she did when I first wrote to you over 17 years ago.

    I am now thirty and a part of three people—two dogs—two birds—two fish and a very fat mouse and I find that time after time I need to dip into Anne's spirit and re-new my own spirit. I miss you both.

    Today was "baby" Jesse's first day at pre-school! He is now 2 years and 4 months old and Ethan is 4 years and 4 months old. They are wild as ever, but so much fun—so zany—so! loving—so TOTAL in their commitment to whatever they are into. I will be glad for my free mornings while they're in school. I plan to continue touring as a docent at the L.A. Zoo and also take a few "animal" classes there and I also hope to continue my writing. I am anxious to balance my life more. I am a much better person to live with when I am feeling peaceful inside. It's a constant goal of mine.

Thankfully, I have Kent to help me out—to back me up. He is an incredible father and the boys adore him—as do I. We all wish we could see you both—we think about you so many times.

8/18/75

My dear friends:

You won't believe how close we came to see you. I wrestled with the idea of even telling you at all about it. We were just that close. Kent was going to shoot a commercial in Switzerland and he said there would be no way he was going to go without me. The whole thing was going to happen last month—he had found out about it on a Friday and we were supposed to be in Europe on Monday. I was in total shock. What to do about the children? My passport? MY GOD!!! My head was a mash of worry and euphoria: the children were so young—who would take care of them and the dogs and the plants—when would I have time to get my passport and if I passed this whole thing up how long would it be before I would embrace *you*—actually *see* you, talk to you in person, drink your wine and/or tea—my knees were weak, my spirit was soaring and I finally concluded that the children and all other lovely spirits that made up the jigsaw picture of our home, would, indeed, make it for the eleven or so days we'd be gone.

And then the whole thing fell thru. Kent ended up in Texas instead and I was full of all kinds of mumble-jumble feelings of relief and despair. My dearest Otto and Fritzi, we know each other so well and yet don't know each other at all. I can't stand not seeing you. At least, send us another recent picture and after we get our developed, I'll send you ours. Isn't that a frustration!? Not a week goes by that I don't think of you. I am now thirty—my boys are four and two and I am finding more time to refind myself even though I am still inundated by a cacophony of dog barks, intermittent screams of joy and anger by the boys as they constantly run and tumble (I've never seen them walk) everywhere and a phone that seems to be timed to ring every time I even approach the typewriter.

Still, I have just finished an article that I hope to see published somewhere—anywhere—so keep your fingers crossed. My greatest high beside this family, however, has been my joyous feat of becoming a docent (teacher-guide) at the Los Angeles Zoo. I take tours of children once a week to meet the animals I can't seem to live without. I am never as happy as when I am around—reading or writing or talking or learning about animals. So after I passed a rigorous four-month course of animal studies at the zoo I have plunged into all the rare and wondrous critters that make up our sorry planet—and once a week at least I can find a solid reason of hope to offer my children. If we give up on our animals and our children—we give up on life. I am convinced they are what life is all about.

I know you have been full of anguish about Israel. I share your agony, believe me. It is almost more than we all can bear seeing and hearing what that feisty, beautiful nation has had to endure. And yet, because of their undaunted passion, I have never felt closer to my people—the biblical people—the Jews. . . .

Kent and I talk about Israel and the tragic babies of a sick, meaningless, shameful Vietnamese war—and of the earth's millions that are dying while others roll in fur coats scraped from the backs of endangered animal species.

Our world is imbalanced. How can people die of hunger while others grow fat? The only things that make any sense—have any dignity, purity, reason for living are the children—and the animals and insects and plants that go on living in spite of the predation around them. How long they will last I hate to think. But as long as they can survive this mess—so can I. . . .

September 8, 1975

Dear Cara,

Summer is nearly over and your letter is still unanswered. But as the New Year started we want to send our best wishes to you and your dear ones.

Though we have no young children and dogs around us we are always quite busy, but of course we have not your juvenile energy any more.

It was sweet of you to send us the lovely photos of your boys. The little one changed a lot. He seems to be more placid whereas Ethan shows a mischievous smile. It is wonderful that they are so near in age that they are company for each other.

A Visit Missed, A Visit Planned—At Last! 99

What a shame that the occasion offered Ken to come to Europe fell through! We too were quite excited when we read about the possibility to see you both here. But now we really hope that you will be able to spend your holidays in Europe taking the boys along.

It was new to us that you are so fond of animals that you took a course to be a teacher-guide in the Zoo. It will interest you to hear that the Basel Zoo is a very famous one, as it has much success in raising young ones of animals which do not give birth in Zoos in general, f.i. gorillas. . . . As you can imagine, we are now a little more optimistic about the situation in Israel. We now have to wait if the agreement reached by Mr. Kissinger will really mean a first step to peace and if it will be kept in the right spirit. Otherwise you are right that the world is in a mess and nobody knows the roots of all the aggression, fanatic nationalism and terrorism. Anyhow we do not despair as we are getting from many decent people so many signs of good will, and this gives us strength.

All the best to you and your dear ones and lots of love . . .

Yours affectionately . . .

November 5, 1975

Dear Cara,

It's time that we are giving you a sign of life again, and to answer your last letter. It really was a strange coincidence that the Schnable book fell to your feet in the book-store. I am very astonished never having mentioned this book to you. In the meantime you will have read it and seen that it is a very important book as it tells about what happened before and after we went into hiding and gives a good background of the time of the occupation of Holland. We went to Amsterdam again and have noticed that the visit to the house does not diminish, on the contrary there were 25% visitors more than last year.

The work of the Foundation continues steadily subsidized by the Government. It consists a.o. in courses for underprivileged groups of the population and seminars for teachers and students of social academies about discrimination and prejudice.

On our way to Amsterdam we stopped in Frankfort to talk to my lawyer on account of an antisemitic slander connected with the Diary. In a book about Hitler it was called a falsification. I succeeded in the meantime to get a court-order to confiscate the book, and I am asking now the publisher to set the matter right in adverts.

Apart from this disagreeable affair we also have nice experiences. We were for 2 days in Geneva to meet the choir of the Japanese Christian friends of Israel; with one of its members I am in correspondence for many years. The choir gave a concert there which we attended singing Japanese and Hebrew songs among which "A Requiem for Anne," a beautiful piece of music. We invited the group to visit us in our home and all 18 members came over and we had a very enjoyable afternoon together. From here they went on to Israel to give concerts there.

We always like the stories you are telling us about your boys. We are surprised that little Jesse is already going to a pre-school, but we understand very well that the 3 free mornings are very welcome to you, so that you have time for the work connected with animals which is giving you a counter-balance to your duties at home.

It is wonderful to know that you and Ken together with the 2 boys form such an island of love in this unrestful world. We still have the hope as the children are now a little older that there will be a possibility to come to Europe so that we finally can meet each other.

All the best and our fondest regards and love to all of you . . .

Dearest Otto and Fritzi—

We received your delicious box of cookies and loved every delicious last crumb! Thank you so much— we'd never tasted anything like them before and they were a treat for all our family and friends over the holiday season! We had to hide them from the boys and only give them a few each day because they were so *crazy* about them! Yummy! We loved that picture you sent us—you both looked so strong and healthy—so beautiful against the backdrop of mountainy snow. I want so much to be with you people!

We hope you had a lovely time with your grand-children over the holidays—we want to extend the invitation to any of your family and/or friends that if any of them are out in California they *must* come and see us . . . Our home is open to any people you love!

In your picture you looked like you both had been skiing. Are you skiers? Kent and I and both *Ethan* and *Jesse* took skiing lessons this holiday—you would have laughed seeing our little boys flying down the little snowy hills in their miniature ski outfits complete with sunglasses! The little guys did a lot better than Kent and I! We had a terrific time and hope to go back soon if our *hot* California winter will hurry up and get cold! We are having a July experience now! It's the hottest winter since 1923!

April 27, 1976

Dear Cara,

. . . Now to your idea about a telephone-call. I agree with you that it would be great to hear each other's voices and hereby to feel close. But I know by experience that I would get very excited and surely would not find the right words. So I think it is better not to follow up this idea.

Little Jesse seems to have inherited his parents artistic qualities being talented in painting. His cards are really interesting and we like them.

For the summer we have not yet any plans, but a number of visitors announced themselves already. We wish you were among them. . . .

10/16/76

My dearest ones:

Kent just sent us a letter—he is still shooting his commercial in Europe, but, hopefully will be back with us by the time you receive this note—he told us how he was able to reach you and speak to you.

A most eery feeling. My own husband talking— actually speaking with the man I have felt was the grandfather I had adopted. He said it was strange for him, too. He wishes so much as do we all, that we could meet. Kent said it was particularly painful for him to visit the Anne Frank House. He signed my name on the registry. He sensed that it was something you did not want to talk about, and commented on how strongly he felt my presence there.

I was talking about Anne recently to a lovely friend of mine and she said that she tries to read Anne's diary at least once a year. She said it always renews her strength and faith in herself and in humankind. I find, the older I get and the more in touch I become with young people, the stronger Anne's spirit courses through my veins. I wish we could arm-in-arm around Basel and talk, Fritzi and Otto. . . .

So, my dearest friends, we continue on: I am finding the boys' school schedule a bit crazy for me and yet good in the sense that it gives me more one-to-one time with each of them: Jesse goes to nursery school in the morning and Ethan goes to kindergarten in the afternoon. What with afterschool classes for Ethan (Chef's class on Tues. and Plant and Animal class on Thursday)—my zoo docentry and classes at least twice a week, plus all the madness of marketing, the bank, post office, etc., etc.,—my foot is never far from the gas pedal. Yet, I am enjoying the boys as never before and am growing into a, hopefully, more mature, calmer individual. I am working very hard to shed my hysteria—my goal is PEACE. Not a bad one to strive for. . . . So, my far-away people, I pray your New Years was a happy, healthful one and that you and your loved ones are well. Much, much love to you both. I promised I will write sooner next time and I hope to hear from you soon!

December 1st, 76.

Dear Cara,

It was a thrill for me too, to talk to Kent and to feel your loving thoughts through him. What a pity you could not come with him, so that we would have had a chance to meet.

I can understand that he felt you near him while visiting the Anne Frank House, knowing your deep involvement for Anne and what she stands for. . . .

Now we are wishing you, Ken and the boys a very happy holiday-season, too, hoping that in 1977 we finally may have the chance to meet you all. Lots of love to the 4 of you. . . .

January 24, 77.

Dear Cara,

We are glad that the cookies finally arrived and that parents and children enjoyed them. We hope that you also received the little book I sent you which contains a little citation from Anne's Diary.

Now I want to thank you for your nice present which arrived safely. We lit the candle when we had my sister and her husband for dinner. . . .

I am quite well again and we went to London for the holiday-season. We had a lovely time with children and grandchildren who were all at home. We saw many friends and relatives who all came to see us, as we did not want to go to town. Our daughter's house is situated in a beautiful district outside London and we could make nice walks. London was full of tourists who took advantage of the low pound to buy cheaper than at home. Now we intend to go to the mountains for a week as a vacation there does us always a lot of good.

We wonder if your hope to meet each other will be realized this year. We don't give up hope. Will you please thank the boys for their drawings which shows the temperament of each of them. It is most rewarding and exciting to follow their spiritual development and we can imagine that their questions can not always be answered easily.

Our nephew who is an actor in Berlin and his wife will probably come to Los Angeles and visit friends there. If their plan will be realized we shall give them your address. His name is Buddy Elias.

Keep well and happy. We are sending *you all* our love. . . .

1977

My dearest Fritzi and Otto!

I can barely believe I am about to say what I am about to say *but*—there is a chance that I may fly out to see you this summer! It's true—Kent & I have talked about nothing else since we started this idea. My dearest Kent wants us to meet NOW & will not allow me to tell him the Reality—that financially I don't know how we can do it & yet he's convinced me that a few weeks on my own, doing something I've dreamed about for almost 18 years can't be such a crime.

It would only be a few days here & there adding up to about two weeks away from the little family I've never been away from—friends in New York, Holland

and *YOU! YOU!* Where will you be in June—July—August? Would it be best to meet in England? I would want to see the Anne Frank Foundation so very much—Am considering late June or mid-July—Please let me know your plans—I will meet you wherever you say—Still can't believe these words—dying to go, yet so afraid to leave. . . . Write soon—Much love . . .

June 6, 1977

Dearest Cara,

Your letter containing the exciting news that you may come over this summer only reached us with delay, as we have been in London for about 3 weeks and did not have our mail forwarded. It would be wonderful to be able to meet finally after so many, many years of correspondence.

Now to our plans for the summer. We arranged with our family to meet in a Swiss mountain-resort from July 14th to the end of the month. Otherwise we have no plans to be away from home. So you can arrange your itinerary accordingly. We understand that you also want to go to Amsterdam to visit the Anne Frank House. There is now an interesting exhibition in the house "Ultra right in Western Europe." You also will see the new statue of Anne which has been unveiled in March.

We are looking forward impatiently to hear at which date we can expect you here. We can imagine that it will mean a great adventure for you to travel alone to Europe for the first time, leaving Kent and the little boys at home.

By the way we just gave your address and tele-phone-number to a nephew Buddy Elias (son of my sister) who is an actor in Berlin. He intends to make a trip to America with his wife, staying a few days in Los Angeles where they have good friends. This will be sometimes in July. He promised to phone you, but if you will be in Europe just then, they will not be able to meet you, but perhaps Ken and the boys. Buddy and his wife are lovely people.

We want this letter to be off and hope to get good news from you soon.

Lots of love to the 4 of you . . .

Through Otto's coaxing, Buddy and his beautiful wife, "Bambi," arrived at our home. The two were traveling the States from Berlin and spent a brief few hours with me. How strange that Buddy should enter my life at that particular time. Somewhere inside, I couldn't help thinking that Anne was planning all this, arranging to bring her friends together.

Over bowls of fresh summer fruit we all talked at once, trying to learn as much about each other as fast as we could. It was a particular joy to meet Buddy, the beloved cousin of Anne Frank. He was very animated, funny, dramatic—burst-ing with life and vitality. His large, dark eyes sparkled with intelligence and warmth. I could easily understand why this vibrant man was an actor. As I watched him laughing and talking, I felt Anne's spirit. I knew that *this* was how Anne truly was. I couldn't wait to ask him about her. "Did you know Anne very well?"

Buddy shot back in his sharp German accent, "Of course! She was my cousin! We were very silly together, prac-tically the same age."

Her *cousin*. I was actually eating cantaloupe with Anne Frank's cousin! "What was she like?"

"A brat!"

"C'mon."

"She was! Also a tease! A practical joker. She wanted to be an ice skater with me, which I was for a while. She would dream of our doing duets on ice together." He laughed, then paused. "She had beautiful, expressive eyes."

Buddy and Bambi were terribly excited about my trip to meet Otto. They had additional plans for me: "You, of course, remember Miep. We will write to her and prepare her for your visit. She will show you around the Anne Frank House herself. You will see it through her eyes."

6/77

My Dearest Otto and Fritzi—

I am so excited I can barely allow myself to think about the trip too much. It's like dreaming about moon—walking or star-floating: so abstract and unbelievable!

I plan to arrive in Zurich from Amsterdam at 11:25 AM via SR 791 on July 30th. I am not sure if I will see you at the airport or should I call you when I arrive? Maybe you could leave a message there at the airport or possibly tell Miep, who I definitely will call upon arrival in Amsterdam (July 27-29—will probably stay at a youth hostel across from the Anne Frank House).

I fell in love with Bambi and Buddy and friend, Pat. They are incredible people and we felt as if we already knew each other—the emotion and conversation were overflowing. I wish we hadn't had such a brief time together.

I thought I'd let you in on my plans while in Basel. How would you like a behind-the-scenes tour of the Basel Zoo? The director of the zoo here in L.A. has promised to send a letter of introduction for me to the Basel director so I can see this most prestigious zoo. I would love to have us all go together! There is so much I want to talk about with you but must save it for LATER! My time in Europe will be fleeting—I leave on August 4 probably from London so we will have to cram our time together in a few, wonderful days. Hug yourselves for me! Much love and kisses . . .

June 29, 1977
Dear Cara,

It was wonderful to speak to you on the phone and to get the confirmation that your plans to come to Europe have taken shape.

We are *very excited* at the prospect to have you here with us, so that we finally shall meet each other personally. As we told you we shall return from our holidays in the mountains on July 28th or 29th and it would be good if you would phone us from Amsterdam the exact date and time of your arrival in Basel. . . .

The best time to call is in the morning between 8 and 9 o'clock or in the evening at about 7. We shall write to Miep about your visit to Amsterdam and ask her to meet you. . . . It would be nice if she could meet you at the Anne Frank House and show you around. We shall mention this idea when we are writing her.

As my wife told you on the phone we shall make reservations for you and your 2 friends here in Birsfelden. (Hotel Alpha) as soon as we know the exact date of your arrival. We want this letter to go off quickly, as we soon will have the occasion to speak about everything personally.

Looking forward very much to your visit we are sending lots of love to you and your dear ones. . . .

A Dream Realized

July 15, 1977

Dear Cara,

We just received your letter and hurry to answer you.

You are asking if we would meet you at the airport, but this is not possible and would be too complicated for us. We advise you to take the Swiss-Air-bus to the terminal which is at the railway-station and take the next train to Basel, which will take about one hour and a quarter.

If you could manage to ring us up from the terminal, this would be the best to do, so that we could meet you at the Basel station.

We do not know who gave you the idea that there is a youth hostel next to the Anne Frank House. This was the case years ago. But of course there are youth hostels in the city.

We were glad to hear, but not astonished that you liked Bambi and Buddy. So do we, otherwise we would not have asked them to get in touch with you.

It was a good idea to ask for an introduction to the Basel Zoo and of course we shall love to go there together.

Just as you are looking forward with great excitement and expectations to meet each other finally.

We appreciate it greatly that you are undertaking this trip to Europe mainly to visit us and . . . we are extremely happy that you can carry out this plan at least and we are grateful to Ken that he agreed.

We are wishing you a good flight and hardly can wait to have you with us.

Lots of love . . .

That was my last letter from Otto before my trip to see him after over twenty years of correspondence. Kent didn't stop encouraging me to "meet Otto Frank now, before it's too late." At the time, Otto was eighty-eight. And I was terrified. This was the first time in my life I was journeying by myself. Up to that point I had never been anywhere alone. Frightening thought. But with my husband's insistence, and his family generously caring for my two little boys in Missouri, I tearfully embraced them all in a fierce first-time-ever good-bye—my little ones, ages five and seven, disappearing into a cluster of relatives. Ethan, the eldest, clung to me a little longer—a few tears mingling with his infectious smile.

Suddenly I was alone in a strange, summer-hot airport, sipping camomile tea and rereading the words of a thirteen-year-old war victim while flies buzzed me from nose to toes and my tea got cold. I had never felt so alone. What in the world had I done? What if Otto wasn't anything like I pictured him to be? What if he just shook my hand and we had a very reserved discussion over some more tea in some strange Swiss restaurant and then I was expected to leave? But where would I go? Where was my family? My Boston connection was announced in the nick of time. I was about to call the whole thing off.

And so my journey began. From California to Missouri to Boston to London on a plane as big as a building, carrying East Indians, Brits, Italians, Americans, and teams of other colorful types. I semi-slept all night as I listened to the wails and whines of other people's children and slowly found myself enjoying my aloneness. Being just me in my own bones, with nobody calling me "Mommy" for the first time in many moons. I continued reading the diary, wrote in my journal, and pondered my trip again.

As Buddy and Bambi had orchestrated it, my pilgrimage to Otto would start in Amsterdam, meeting Miep and Jan. Anne mentioned the incredible Miep many times in her writings—she was Otto's loyal secretary, the non-Jew who was one of the key lifelines for the Jews hiding in the annex above the office of the spice factory where Miep worked.

Miep would seek out sympathetic friends, also non-Jews, who would set aside extras: food, clothes, books, etc., for her without ever asking for what they were needed. She and Jan, her husband, had just been married when the Franks had to go into hiding. The tension and anxiety they all went through would prevent the couple from being able to conceive. It would be more than five years after the war before their only child, Paul, was born to the middle-aged couple.

Buddy's words still echoed in my mind. "You, of course, remember Miep. We will write to her and prepare her for your visit. She will show you around the Anne Frank House herself. You will see it through her eyes."

The Amsterdam airport was glistening wet, looking like so many foreign films. To add to the drama, one piece of luggage was lost. As much as I love to think of myself going it alone, I actually didn't entirely. I was met by two wonderful Dutch friends, Ellen and Girard.

Their car soon had me in front of the neat little brick apartment building that was Miep's home. I checked the address, and soon I was entering the tiny apartment and shaking hands at last with Miep—the lovely Viennese woman who had reluctantly become famous through Anne Frank. She was a strong, short woman, sixty-nine years old then, with light-blond hair and a direct, no-nonsense air about her.

"Hello, I am Miep. And this"—she turned to the tall, lanky, white-haired Dutchman—"is Jan." (In the diary, Anne had referred to Jan as "Henk," one of a great many people's names, Miep explained later, that had been disguised for their protection. The young girl had planned for the diary's publication someday, but that is a later story. . . .)

The couple shyly and in a halting mix of English, Dutch, and German arranged to meet me the next day at the Anne Frank House. Later I said good-bye to Ellen and Girard, after much discussion over what, indeed, were my plans. We decided to meet again the following week. I would return to their little city of Groningen after my mission was accomplished. Now I was again on my own. A strange feeling for a very sheltered, twenty-four-hour-a-day Mommy. Very strange, indeed.

The next day the cab driver dropped me off at Prinsengracht 263. I stood outside the tall, narrow brick building and stared. Bicyclists sped by. Tourists snapped away. Houseboats bobbed gently along the canal. And I stood statuelike in front of the looming specter that had once housed and hidden Anne Frank. A click and buzz of the door, a long, steep climb up endless stairs into the main office. People everywhere. Leaflets and books and glass-encased articles and newspaper clipping—examples of racism and universal persecution. A guest book fat with the signatures of people from around the globe. I looked out from the ceiling-high front windows down to the cobblestone street below.

I'm sitting cozily in the main office, looking outside through a slit in the curtain. It is dusk but still just light enough to write you. It is a very queer sight, as I watch the people walking by; it looks just as if they are all in a terrible hurry and nearly trip over their toes. With cyclists, now, one simply can't keep pace with their speed. I can't even see what sort of person is riding on the machine.
(*Anne*, The Diary)

An elderly couple in matching beige raincoats stood elegantly waiting below. I tapped on the glass and waved. They looked up and waved back and entered the building. Miep, once again, was in the Frank House.

"Will this be painful for you, Miep?"

She put her arm in mine briskly, and I took up her stride. "No, Cara, I have been here many times. Though it hasn't been for a while. I have yet to meet the new director. No, I am really fine."

The students behind the counter shook hands with the couple. They had recognized Miep and were genuinely pleased to see her. Jan was always by her side. He seemed to balance this volatile lady with the fire still burning in her eyes. As she talked to me, her voice carried above the hum of the crowd.

Little clusters of the curious began trailing us. ("Who is that woman?" "How does she know so much about this place?") I wondered if maybe Miep wasn't aware that she was becoming a focal point. There was a bit of the performer in her. She always seemed to speak with a great sense of the dramatic.

You couldn't ever doubt her. She demanded your immediate trust and attention. I doubled my steps to keep pace with her. And the tour was under way.

"This," she said, circling one room, "used to be my

office. I sat right there, Elli, over there, and Mr. Koophuis right there. Over there is where Mr. Kraler and Mr. Van Daan worked." It was like a scene from *Our Town*.

We walked up some more steep stairs to another creaking landing. I tried to ignore the flashbulbs popping around me, the ticket takers, the crush of people—always the people when you most wanted to be alone. I focused on the past, and everyone else didn't matter.

Miep pulled me on. "We cannot use those wooden steps anymore. Not safe." She pointed to a covered grating at our feet. "But those were the original steps we took to get from the office to here." We walked through a narrow passageway leading from an unobtrusive-looking gray door that doubled as a bookshelf. Up another steep stairway and we were there. Inside "the secret annex."

I took a deep breath, hoping to inhale some history. It smelled too clean. Miep pointed to a freshly painted wall. "This use to be their closet, right here." She bent over the miniature model of the annex and described it the way she remembered it so vividly:

"Here is where Anne would write in her diary. Right here by the window. In the room where we stand. I remember once taking a picture of her as she was writing. She looked up at me, slammed her book shut, and stormed out of the room. She was very angry with me for doing that. Yes, she had a temper.

"But she also loved to laugh and talk all the time, too. When I would enter the room after giving my special knock, they would all be standing silent, expectant, fearful, excited to see me, to hear what I had to say. No one would say a thing. Except, of course, Anne. She would rush up to me and immediately want to know, 'Well, Miep, what's the news? What's happening?' She was a lovely child. Very fragile looking with large, expressive eyes."

Sometimes I believe that God wants to try me, both now and later on; I must become good through my own efforts, without examples and without good advice. Then later on I shall be all the stronger. Who besides me will ever read these letters? (Anne, The Diary)

We walked from one tiny area to the next. The room where Anne slept with her terrible pain of a roommate, the dentist Dussel. The washbasin and tiny W.C. Up another flight of creaky stairs to the Van Daan's quarters and the communal kitchen. "This is where they would listen to the radio," she said.

Jan nodded. "Yes, I would spend many hours visiting with them all listening to the radio together—right here."

Miep pointed around the room. "There was a cupboard here. And this table here is where they all sat and ate. Anne would sit here. Mrs. Frank here. Mr. Frank here. Margot here. No, no, Peter would sit here and Margot here. Mr. Pfeffer ["Dussel"], was it here? No right here. Mr. and Mrs. Van Pels ["Van Daans"] over there and there.

"And it was right here"—she pointed so dramatically and with such impact that a chill shot through me and the little band of people who followed us stood silent, clinging to her words—"right here is where I found *The Diary.*"

I stared at the place on the floor, hoping that some vestigial aura would still be there. Miep and Bep ("Elli") had returned to the annex after the Gestapo, in the form of the Dutch police, had taken its occupants away. When Miep discovered the piles of papers and books strewn all over the floor, she had gathered them quickly and put them in a safe until the time when, she hoped, the family would be released to claim them.

"I never read a word on those papers. It was a blessing that I didn't. Fate, really. Because *had* I read Anne's manuscripts, her diary, her stories, I would most assuredly have burned them all. She had mentioned too many names. She was actually in the process of changing our names [hence Jan became Henk; Bep, Elli; van Pels, Van Daans; Pfeffer, Dussel]. A lot of people's lives would have been greatly endangered. It was fate I didn't read those papers. . . ."

The tourists could contain themselves no longer. The questions burst through the air. Who was she? Miep answered them all, and turning to each cluster of followers she would exclaim, "Did you read *The Diary*? Well, I am Miep of *The Diary* and"—she would point proudly to her shy Jan—"this is Henk!" The place went crazy. Everyone crowded around her, asking for autographs, grabbing her hands, taking her picture, smiling through misty eyes, staring in disbelief. "Miep, of *The Diary*" was actually there. I knew how they felt.

As Miep and Jan talked to the crowd, I walked into the next little room. Peter's room. Peter, the beautiful teenager who was the subject of many romantic passages in Anne's diary. I remember falling in love with Peter right along with Anne. The handsome adolescent who once studied, brooded, fumed, daydreamed, cried, and loved in this very room.

An ancient wooden step led from Peter's room to a small entryway in the ceiling. It was roped off at the top so you could only climb up and peer into the darkness. The attic. Anne would spend many hours alone up here. Writing. Staring out the window. Catching the feel of fresh air and a glimpse of the seasons. The outside.

> *The sun is shining, the sky is a deep blue, there is a lovely breeze and I'm longing—so longing—for everything. To talk, for freedom, for friends, to be alone. And I do so long . . . to cry! I feel as if I'm going to burst, and I know that it would get better with crying; but I can't, I'm restless, I go from one room to the other, breathe through the*

crack of a closed window, feel my heart beating, as if it is
saying, "Can't you satisfy my longings at last?"
I believe that it's spring within me, I feel that spring
is awakening, I feel it in my whole body and soul. It is an
effort to behave normally, I feel utterly confused, don't
know what to read, what to write, what to do, I only
know that I am longing. . . . (Anne, The Diary)

Later, Peter would join her and they would hold each other.

I loved the fact that we couldn't enter this special sanctuary. I imagined that the balls of dust and lacy cobwebs held some of the past. It smelled old and damp. Perfect.

Miep broke away from the group. She gestured to a little ledge outside the window of Peter's room—to a tiny wrought-iron balcony. "Peter and Anne would spend many nights right here. Just holding hands. Whispering. Very quiet."

We walked back to the entrance. Miep and Jan continued signing autographs, posing for pictures. The director, Cornelis Sujik, wanted to meet them for a chat, some tea. Would they come to his office, please? I joined them for a while, enjoying the theatricality of their animated conversation—all in Dutch. After a while I excused myself, explaining I'd meet them later. I wanted to see a bit of Amsterdam, the canals, the street that Anne was so desperate to be a part of. As I walked, I began feeling very Dutch myself, loving the sound of my feet on the worn cobblestone—and the sad, faraway chime of Anne's Westertoren clock.

Daddy, Mummy, and Margot can't get used to the
sound of the Westertoren clock yet, which tells us the time
every quarter of an hour. I can. I loved it from the start,
and especially in the night it's like a faithful friend.
(Anne, The Diary)

Miep and Jan were just coming out of the building. She swept her arm into mine and once again I was two-stepping to keep up with her. We hopped in a cab; its windshield wipers beat like a metronome keeping a cadence to our conversation. I turned to Miep with a question.

"How is it, Miep, that when the Dutch or Green Police came for the Jews that you, too, weren't captured? After all, you were an obvious accomplice."

She smiled conspiratorially and tapped my arm. "Oh, that is quite a story. I will tell you when we are home." This was definitely going to be good. After jumping out of the cab (was there anything *slow* about this lady?!) we practically skipped to their little apartment. Finally, warm and dry, we sat in the immaculate front room. Doilies and lovely European artifacts, prints on the wall, a loudly ticking clock. Miep settled into the couch. Jan sat facing us. The story would begin now.

"The day it happened, you know, I was at my desk in the main office. I rememember the door being opened and these officers from the Green Police [Dutch working for the gestapo] were there. The main officer came over to Mr. Kraler, the office manager, and said very quietly, 'Where are the Jews? We know they are here, so just take me to them now.' He had a gun and his eyes seemed to look through us. He knew. Someone had told them.

"With them following Kraler, they led him to the bookshelf. Then they started pounding away, tearing down books, finally discovering the latch to the door; they climbed into the annex. The family reacted quietly, like in a trance. They put some of their clothes into bags. No talking.

"When the officer found Otto's German military footlocker and realized this Jew had once been an important German officer, the Nazi was really shocked. He almost saluted. Kept saying over and over again, 'Don't rush. Take your time. Take your time.' I was standing behind my desk. He pointed the barrel of the gun straight at me. I will never forget that feeling. 'Now it is your turn.' I stared back at him. You see, I had recognized his accent. He wasn't Dutch but, rather, Viennese, like myself.

"With the gun still pointed at my face, I answered him. 'But, you're from Vienna. So am I.' Well, the man went crazy. After all, here was this woman who was from his homeland. It shocked him. He started pacing the room like a caged animal. Shouting at me. 'Shame on you for hiding Jews!' I said nothing. 'What am I going to do with you? What do you think I should do with you?' I still said nothing. Just stared back at him.

"Finally, he came back over to me. 'All right. I will not do anything right now. You will continue to work here and you must not ever leave town. I will come and check on you and make sure you are here. If you dare leave, I will take away your man.'"

Miep winced in pain. She practically whispered the words, "Then I said a stupid thing: 'He knows nothing! My husband knows nothing.' But, thank God, the officer didn't question me any more. And he did come and check on me many times. Never said anything. Just made sure I was there."

Countless friends and acquaintances have gone to a terrible fate. Evening after evening the green and gray army lorries trundle past. The Germans ring at every front door to inquire if there are any Jews living in the house. If there are, then the whole family has to go at once. If they don't find any, they go on to the next house. No one has a chance of evading them unless one goes into hiding. Often they go around with lists, and only ring when they know they can get a good haul. Sometimes they let them off for cash—so much per head. It seems like the slave hunts of olden times. But it's certainly no joke; it's much too tragic for that. In the evenings when it's dark, I often see rows of good, innocent people accompanied by

crying children, walking on and on, in charge of a couple of
these chaps, bullied and knocked about until they almost drop.
No one is spared—old people, babies, expectant mothers, the sick—
each and all join in the march of death. (Anne, The Diary)

The clock in the room ticked louder. Miep excused herself to prepare dinner, and Jan and I talked about their son, Paul. The tall, reserved Dutchman mellowed when he talked about his child.

The silver and china glistened as we sat for dinner. The formal setting was very natural to them. So very European and right. I found myself missing my grandmother—the fiery Hungarian lady, Gizella, whose own apartment and table and general style were not unlike Miep's. How many times had I sat at Grandma's perfect table just like this. . . .

Miep's story wasn't finished. She would tell me how she and Jan still didn't give up. They went to the baker and the grocer and many other brave Dutch people. This time Miep asked them for money to try to bribe the Nazis into releasing the Franks and Van Daans and Dussel. There had been cases where such bribes did work. So, Miep gathered the money together, went straight to gestapo headquarters, walked right up to the same portly Viennese officer who had pointed the gun at her face, and without saying a word, circled her thumb against her fingers in the universal symbol meaning "money."

He shook his head. "It won't work anymore. Too late. They are already gone. Anyway, it won't work." (The good old days of excess were dwindling. Hitler's regime was weakening.)

Miep stared back at him. "I don't believe you." The Nazi pointed upstairs. "Go and talk to my superiors if you don't believe me. But I tell you it won't work anymore." So Miep charged up the stairs, opened the door.

There sitting around a table was a group of Nazis intently listening to the English radio. They bolted straight when they saw her. They screamed, "Get out! Get out!" Miep turned and walked down the stairs past the Viennese officer.

"I told you so." She kept walking and closed the door behind her—and, with it, hope for her friends.

Our dinner was finished. Miep and Jan cleared the table and insisted I shouldn't help. I was their guest. Then they reappeared, carrying dishes of deliciously cool yogurt with fresh summer fruit. The conversation continued. I was curious about Otto—and very anxious to see him. I knew that he was the sole survivor of the little band of Jews from the annex. Where did he go once back from the concentration camp?

"He came to us. To Jan and me. He was deeply depressed. Very, very nervous. But he had lots of friends to visit and offer his help. He was constantly involved in reuniting displaced concentration camp victims with their friends and families.

"He always found someone who needed support. He also was very involved in Anne's diary. It took him months to read all of it. It was terribly painful for him," Miep said. "He stayed with us for seven years. But we didn't really see that much of him. He was busy every minute. He even returned to work in the spice factory he had managed below the annex. Fritzi was also in his life. She, too, was a war victim, and life was happier for Otto because of her. He took great pleasure in our baby, Paul. He loved him very much. You will love Otto. He is a wonderful man."

The talk of Otto made me restless. It was becoming evening and I would have to leave very early in the morning to catch a plane for Switzerland, and my ultimate destination. Miep and Jan put on their matching raincoats and took my arm. They would accompany me on the tram back to my hotel. I felt so close to these two incredible people. On the tram, I turned to Miep and held her hand tightly. I told her how proud I was to know her. Women, especially, must know her story—must learn of her courage. It would inspire them.

They would share my pride in a woman who didn't give up fighting. Miep shook her head. She wanted no praise.

"Cara, what else could I do? Anybody would have done the same. You just do what you have to do. That's all."

The tram stopped at my hotel. My new, buttoned-down friends embraced me. I looked into their faces. I never wanted to forget them. War heroes. I gave them another hug, and then they were gone.

I stood for a moment in the lobby, trying to gain some perspective. I felt terribly heavy and serious inside. I hadn't really laughed or been silly for much too long. I talked to the young people working behind the desk. One girl had a craving for a special kind of chocolate Lindt bar. I wanted some magazines with lots of pictures and no heavy reading. I told her I would try to find her candy if she would just point the way.

I found my spirits lifting and my youth returning as I walked the twilight streets of downtown Amsterdam. Young people, longhairs, embracing lovers, curbside musicians; rowdy types next to the beautiful and privileged next to scraggly students—there was a street tapestry weaving around me, lifting me back to the present. I felt lighter. And then the butterflies returned to my stomach. Tomorrow I would be in the clouds once again. Tomorrow I would meet Otto Frank.

In the morning, a plane lifted me toward Switzerland. Then a bus got me to the train depot. I lugged with me two huge, unnecessary albatrosses—the suitcases I was warned by everybody not to burden myself with.

And now here I was on the train. Too exhausted to drag those tons of clothes through car after car, I knew I'd never reach third class, my destination. I collapsed in a pool of sweat in a corner near a window, and since all the seats in the car were filled, I sat on my bulging suitcases. And listened. Bits of animated conversation surrounded me in French,

Dutch, German. And watched. A monastery rushed by my view. Glimpses of the Rhine here and there. A blink of a bridge spanning from one bank to the other. Church spires pushed through clumps of forest. Barges hauled their weighty cargo through the still water.

I leaned my head against the cool window glass as the rhythmic clacking lulled me into a dreamy state. I thought of trains. How ironic that they seemed to be a strange link in this story. The holocaust death trains taking the victims to the camps. The trains returning the survivors to their lives. And this train taking me to one of the most famous survivors in the world. I practiced how it was going to be when we met. Of course I wanted it to be all emotion, embraces, tears. But that was *my* script. Life—as I was constantly learning—didn't always conform to the scenes in my head. No, Otto would probably shake my hand quite formally, a little shyly, and we would have a very civilized time together, and then that would be that. I hated the scenario, but I was prepared.

Then I heard it. The conductor distinctly said, "Basel!" There. He'd said it again. It wasn't a dream. I stood up and rubbed my numb behind, which felt as though it had the indentation of suitcase handles and tags forever branded on it. The postcard backdrops had disappeared and Basel Station screeched into view.

Doors flew open. A mass of pushing and shoving. I staggered into the middle of a buzzing swarm of humanity, hundreds of passengers trying to get out and in at the same time. A handsome young German took pity on me as I struggled with my unrelenting luggage. He grabbed the bags and got me onto the platform.

I looked into the crowd of people and saw her immediately. She looked exactly like her pictures. Fritzi! At once I was hugging and kissing this tall, striking-looking woman. In her strong German accent she said, "Cara, I thought you were shorter from your pictures next to Kent!"

"Oh, I am, Fritzi; it's just the sandals. They add a lot of inches!"

"Where's your luggage?

"Right over there; oh, don't try to pick them up. They're far too heavy, believe me! Where's Otto?"

"Over there, see him? He is looking for you."

Oh God. He *was* right over there. That beautiful man with the straight back and Lincolnesque face. The chisled features. High, carved cheekbones and snow-white hair around a balding head. The skin a patchwork of dark and light pigmentation. A very tall, elderly man. Still so strong and handsome. Large hands. A black overcoat. A hint of a white shirt and tie. It was really him. Otto Frank.

"Cara! At last!"

I was actually hugging him. A real bear hug. Thank God. No formal handshakes. No polite hellos. We pulled away and stared at each other. Suddenly a little shy, he put his arm in mine. Fritzi linked my other arm and we walked off into the sunset, the music swelling as the credits rolled. No, Cara, no, no, no! This was not a movie, not a dream, not even a daydream. This was real, unscripted *life*.

I snuggled close to my beloved bookends and found myself scrunched into a taxi and then swooshed out in front of my new "home" in Basel. The Hotel Alpha. A beautiful relic from a long ago time. My room was as tiny as it was crisp and immaculate. A toy room from a thirties dollhouse. A little box of Swiss chocolates on the desk at the foot of my bed. A gift from Fritzi and Otto.

"Do you like it, Cara?"

I loved it. But I was ready to take the tram to their street. It was just a short run. I could easily walk to their house; that's why they had picked that hotel. Their home was so small, they told me. It was uncomfortable to have guests in such close quarters. They hoped I understood. I did, and was very happy with my private retreat down the street.

As we walked, linked arm in arm, I looked up at the

street sign. There it was. The street I had written down on so many, many envelopes through the years. It was real, too. And it pointed to the most immaculate, silent, beautiful old street I'd ever walked on. The homes, three-storied, square-shaped, elegantly subdued in their austerity, surrounded by walls and hedges. We pushed open the iron gate leading to the Franks' home. Otto unlocked the front door while I took in the aroma of rain-fresh flora. They said the people living upstairs did all the gardening. The Franks preferred this duplex arrangement because the neighbors cared for the Franks' home in their many absences.

After Otto had unlocked the front door we went inside and walked up wooden stairs to a platform where another door awaited unlocking. The smells of age and coats and a basement somewhere and heated air brought back a child-hood memory—a hotel-lobby kind of smell. Now it was Fritzi's turn to unlock and slide open this second door. It was a routine that seemed to be understood and unquestioned.

And now we were inside. I was "home." Rich, dark colors, lots of browns and maroons and earth-toned hues like aged tapestry. Pillows and little sculptures and prints and books and doilies. Under every object there was a delicate lace doily, white filigree amid the browns.

Fritzi opened up a cabinet and picked out a few objects, a paperweight, a sculpture. She saw that I didn't recognize them. "You've forgotten these? These are what you sent us many years ago. We keep them here."

I hadn't remembered them at first. They'd been sent so very long ago by a long-ago me. While Fritzi disappeared into the kitchen, Otto took my arm and ushered me outside to a little covered patio and a couch with table and chairs among sweet peas and potted plants. A cozy place without fencing, an entry to the backyard, where there were more plants, trees, a tangled vine of shiny blackberries. Otto searched to find the plumpest ones to pick and hand to me. We ate blackberries together.

He showed me the roses. Everywhere roses. And over there, the most special rose of all: the fragile orange and pink "Anne Frank Rose," created by an admirer in her memory.

Fritzi reappeared with a little wooden tray filled with a lunch spread. And then they took me into their little study. It was there that the two answered the volumes of daily correspondence. A pile of fresh, as yet unopened mail lay stacked on Otto's desk. The elderly man showed me the wall-to-wall notebooks bursting with letters from people all over the world. "And here is where we answer them all, Fritzi and me!"

Two typewriters in two corners of the room. A few pictures, prints on the wall. A sketch of Anne. Another chest filled with mementos from friends and travels. Family photos. A plump pillow tucked into the couch—with names of Anne Frank Club members embroidered in all colors decorating both sides. It was made by a Danish girl, Mette. (Mette later married and had a daughter she named Anne.)

"Cara, you are not the only one to write me all these years. There are many, many like you."

Of course. Why should I be the only one to adopt Otto? I was intrigued. Who were the others? Fritzi and Otto smiled as the names and faces of this uniquely international "family" came to mind.

There was Sumi, from Japan. Sumi lost her father when she was just three years old. Her mother put the child in a nunnery, where she was converted to Catholicism. As a young girl, Sumi read Anne's *Diary* and was moved to write to Otto. She told Otto that since he had lost his two daughters and she had lost her father, could she become his "letter-daughter"—and signed all her letters "your daughter, Sumi." Otto advised her through the years, as he did me. She, too, did what he told her to do. Once she graduated from college as an English major, Sumi looked for work, responding to an ad from Twentieth Century–Fox requesting a secretary fluent in the English language. Sumi gathered all her correspondence from Otto and, accompanied by a nun, introduced herself. The corporation, impressed by her longstanding relationship with the father of Anne Frank, gave the young woman the prestigious position. Otto and Fritzi had already met the lovely Japanese woman and showed me a picture of the three of them smiling together.

There was the young man, Ryan, from Carmel, California. He'd had a lonely life. He and his mother lived a meager existence. Ryan was a dropout from school—a dropout from everywhere. A true lost soul. When his mother died, she left him their tiny house. Ryan was completely alone. And then someone gave him Anne's *The Diary of a Young Girl* to read.

Ryan had been a boy with no intellectual life, not a reader; his only real talent was his ability to draw. He sketched everything. After reading the book, he told Otto and Fritzi in his first letter that his life had changed. This young girl, Anne Frank, had reached him, talked to him, given him something he'd never had before: hope. He became obsessed. He had to meet Otto. He had to go to Amsterdam and see the Anne Frank House.

He sold his house and, with around seven thousand dollars, left immediately for Amsterdam. Once there, he begged the director of the Anne Frank House for a job. He not only wanted to work in the House, he wanted to live there. When he was refused because he wasn't a citizen of Holland, and because living in the House was an impossibility, the desperate youth stayed nearby as long as his money held out. He started to sketch everything. People. The canals. The countryside. And, of course, the Anne Frank House. I saw his exquisite works in both Miep's house and in the Franks'. They looked like old prints. Ryan became an extremely successful illustrator working for a large publishing firm.

Then there was Barbara, a devout Jew who had been writing to "Uncle Otto" and "Aunt Fritzi" for many years as well. She brought her husband to meet the Franks on her honeymoon. Barbara now lives in New York with her family and lectures on Anne Frank to school groups, to Jewish organizations, to all who will listen. Otto and Fritzi were quite proud of Barbara. "She is spreading Anne's spirit."

The Franks had been corresponding with many Russian youths, but found the frustrations of censorship too great. Many times the letters would never reach their destination. Otto no longer wrote to them because he couldn't maintain an honest communication.

John Neiman was a college student in 1974. That's when he reread *The Diary of Anne Frank,* and became so inspired that he wrote to Otto. Two years later, John flew to Switzerland and met Otto and Fritzi in person. The deep friendship was sealed and John became a close friend to the Franks and to Miep and Jan as well. Then in 1979, John had a profound discussion with Otto in London. What Otto had said to the young man—who was so deeply moved by Anne's story—was something that changed the entire course of his life. The elderly man advised, "If you really want to honor Anne's memory and the people that died, you do what Anne wanted so very much to do—do good for other people."

For John, a devout Catholic convert, that meant becoming a priest. Otto Frank had spent the remainder of his life after the war sacrificing his time, always being available to others—and John Neiman decided to follow Otto's example. Neiman joined the seminary the year after their discussion. (Six years after Otto's death, John became a priest. Miep and Jan flew to Los Angeles for Father John Neiman's ordination. As John also was, and still is, a dear friend of mine, I, too, was invited to that most memorable occasion. Today, Father John, a priest for a Redondo Beach, California, parish, continues to reach out to a huge network of Holocaust survivors; lectures frequently on every aspect of Anne and her family and the Holocaust; and remains in close contact with Fritzi and Miep—visiting them at least once a year.)

And then there was that wonderful girl, Vassa. An incredible story. Some time ago, Otto had received a letter written in Greek, from a young Athens girl. In order to understand the letter, Otto went to the Greek embassy, where he was referred to a local Greek teacher. It was she who translated the letter and subsequent letters for him. This young girl, Vassa, told Otto about her horrifying background—how her father, who had been in the underground movement when Greece was occupied by Germany, had been caught, tortured, and murdered in front of Vassa and her mother. Deeply depressed, the young girl lost interest in everything—in her studies, in life itself. Then one day she read in the paper that the play *The Diary of Anne Frank* was to be performed at the local theater. Even though she'd never heard or read about Anne before, Vassa was intrigued by the play's description—the sad life and ultimate death of this young war victim. After seeing the play, Vassa read Anne's book, and then wrote to Otto. And as we all seemed to do, Vassa poured out her heart to this faraway father figure—Otto Frank. His response to Vassa reinforced the point that though Anne was deprived of seeing her goals achieved, dying as young as she did, Vassa had a whole lifetime of hope and promise before her. The correspondence continued for several months, and with Otto's constant encouragement, Vassa overcame her depression and finished her studies at school. Realizing that Vassa no longer needed his advice, Otto wrote to her explaining that it was too much strain having to translate her letters. He was getting too old and had limited time with his demanding schedule. He had to stop writing to her.

For over a year Otto didn't hear from Vassa. Then a letter came signed with her familiar signature. The letter was in French—a language that Otto could speak and read quite fluently. During those months, Vassa studied the French language so that she could continue corresponding with her dear mentor, Otto Frank.

(Later, Vassa was to become a French high school teacher, marry, and have two children—a boy and a girl named Anne. Otto and Fritzi once visited the family in their northern Athens home.)

There were so many more of "Otto's children," too numerous to recount. The young Yugoslavian girl, Ljuba, whose boyfriend became so jealous of her correspondence with Otto that he threatened to kill her! Fortunately, she married another man, much to Fritzi and Otto's relief.

And Teti—the second Greek girl to adopt Otto. She, too, wrote to Otto in French after reading Anne's *Diary.* Teti told Otto how her parents reproached her for being a factory worker, while they had far more respect for her sister, who worked for a radio station. Otto answered that no work is insignificant if you do it well. But he also encouraged her to try to "get a more important job." She did just that. She soon was chosen to represent her company at a fair in Munich. She was quite pleased.

One stormy evening, at ten o'clock, the Franks' bell rang. Opening the door, they found a young girl standing there drenched and shivering. Her teeth chattering, she practically whispered, "I am Teti."

After they gave her warm clothes and a hot meal, Teti told them that she didn't want to go home. Could she stay with the Franks and try to find some work in Basel? She was welcome to stay, and Otto promptly said he'd try to help her, though it wouldn't be easy since she spoke no German.

Off he went again to the Greek consulate, asking for the address of local Greek citizens. Soon he found the perfect situation for Teti: a Greek family with two children, who were eager to have Teti live with them and help with their French and English homework lessons.

When Teti wrote to her parents about her new teacher/ au pair position, they were quite impressed with her. The young Greek girl stayed with the Basel family for more than half a year, visiting Otto and Fritzi often. She learned German, and even dated Otto's nephew, Stephan.

Finally, she returned home, and gratefully found her parents received her with new respect. Teti married an officer —a man she had known long before she left Greece—and had a son. The Franks visited Teti and her family in Athens, and the correspondence continued even after Teti's husband (many years older than she) had died.

The little office was packed with notebooks filled with these letters from Otto's global family. "I receive most of my letters from America. But can you guess from which country I receive almost as many letters?" I rattled off a few guesses, all of them wrong. Otto's eyes twinkled. There was still mischief within him. He answered me in his sort of German-British voice. (He would say "half" and "can't" just like an Englishman.) "Most of the young people we hear from are Japanese!"

The Japanese people identified with Anne's persecution. They related her Holocaust experience to the horrors of atomic warfare in their own past. Otto told of the Japanese Christian youth group he introduced himself to in Israel. They were observing some ruins there, and Otto came over to them and welcomed them to Israel, telling them at the same time that he was the father of Anne Frank. When they heard that they started shouting and crying and putting gifts into his hands and hugging him.

As he recounted the story, Otto's eyes filled. He took out his handkerchief and blew his nose. It was the only time I would see him break down. These young people were an extension of Anne. It was the joy in the present that brought tears to this sweet man, not the bitterness of the past. He was like a father/grandfather to us all.

The entire Japanese Christian youth group that Otto and Fritzi had met in Israel later found its way to Basel. All of the members crowded into the same front room where the three of us sat now. One of the young men in the group became a Christian minister. Today, Reverend Makato Otsuka is working to create the first Holocaust Museum in Hiroshima, Japan. He says that meeting Otto and Fritzi in Israel in 1971 totally "changed my life."

I felt so close to all these people. I knew they were but

a small part of Otto's universal family. I now have this great desire to meet my other "brothers" and "sisters" around the world. We are from all different races and religions, but in one way we are the same. After all, were we not sent by Anne to keep her father company?

Throughout the weekend we would dine at Fritzi's beautiful table and eat the delicious vegetarian meals she went out of her way to prepare for me, knowing my proclivity for nonmeat meals. We would talk, eat, talk some more, and then I would walk back to my little hotel while Otto would nap. I love the memory of my first night there. I hugged them good night and, borrowing their umbrella, I walked back alone through the little town of Birsfelden, next to Basel. A warm summer rain pounded around me. The streets were glossy and crowded with weekend tourists, retreating from their rained-out escapes. An accordian squeezed out a distant melody from somewhere inside a cozy little restaurant. I wrung myself out in my tiny hotel room, then set myself to writing in my journal and on my postcards home: "My first Saturday in Basel, Switzerland. Today, I met Otto Frank."

In the morning we had to get a lot of good talking in before Otto's nap, because afterward we were going to the Basel Zoo! The then-director at the Los Angeles Zoo, Dr. Warren Thomas, had sent a letter of introduction for me, enabling us to get a behind-the-scenes tour of one of the world's most exquisite zoos! (I was a docent at the L.A. Zoo and would become a part-time animal keeper on my return from Europe.)

The morning was going fast and there was so much more I wanted to know. We talked about Anne, looked through the family album that Anne had put together, her neat lettering captioning each photo. Margot powdering baby Anne's bottom. Cousin Buddy and Anne as children. More family. And there was one picture of some beautiful blond-haired moppets playing together in a backyard. They had posed during a brief interval in their game of hide-and-seek, still scruffy with curls aflutter and cheeks flushed. Even in black and white they seemed to glow, smiling shyly at their intruder. Cherubs at play. "You see these children, Cara?" Otto ran his finger across each face. "These were my playmates when I was a boy. And they all became—except that one right there—they all became Nazis."

I was riveted. It was hard to believe. No. Not those sweet babies. I wanted to freeze time. Hold my hand over their faces. Yell at them not to grow up. But they did. They grew up to kill other babies and mothers and fathers. Reality. Nazis were once babies, too.

I sat back in my chair. My eyes traveled from the photo album to the tablecloth, from the fruit and cheese to Fritzi's arm in repose in front of her. Dark purple-black numbers were tattooed deep into the elderly woman's flesh. She caught my stare. "Yes, Cara, these are from the concentration camp. See Otto's?"

The gentle old man rolled up his sleeve. More numbers. I had never seen anything like this before. So ugly. So terribly sad. Humans branding humans.

Fritzi's voice broke the silence. "I had been in hiding, too, Cara. With my husband and son and daughter." She brought over a small oil painting. It was the work of her son before he and his father were taken away. She never saw either of them again. Fritzi and her daughter, Eva, were in the camps together. They survived by caring for each other, by being alive for each other. After the humiliation of being shaved from head to pubis, and living like subhumans, they made it to freedom together.

Through brimming eyes, Fritzi recalled the first moment she met Otto. They had been on the same cattle train from the camps, and as they all poured out onto the platform her daughter pointed excitedly to the gaunt man standing alone. "Look, Mama! There is the father of the girl I used to play with down the street! Anne Frank!"

They had lived across the way from each other for years

and Fritzi and Otto had never even met. Only their daughters had been friends. From the moment they met, the two saw each other constantly. For seven years they courted. Fritzi didn't want to leave Amsterdam until her daughter was married. After being assured by her Israeli future son-in-law that he would never take her daughter to far-away Israel, Fritzi had to relinquish her hold on the child who was life itself to her. Fritzi married Otto and left with him for Basel—and a new life. (The daughter is now a successful antiques dealer living in England with her husband. They have three daughters, and now grandchildren. The children were a constant source of joy to the elder Franks. They were renewed hope for Otto.)

It was time for Otto's nap. Before I left, he brought out another notebook. "Read these, Cara. These are your letters to me. I saved them all." I couldn't believe it. Over twenty years of history. He had saved twenty years of me. I scanned through the huge pile of correspondence and saw my large handwritten scrawl evolve into more adult script, and then change to countless typewritten pages. Masses of exclamation points and underlinings. Outpourings of feelings I didn't remember expressing. I was facing myself through these letters. Otto had saved my youth in more ways than one. . . .

The rest of the day was a dream come true for me. But I'm afraid it was a rather exhausting one for poor Otto. Strong and spry Fritzi seemed to enjoy herself as much as I did. Basel Zoo! We were met by Dr. Studer, the gentle assistant director, who took us behind the scenes of that world-famous wildlife compound. An exquisite zoo. In the warm summer rain we would leave dear Otto quietly catching his breath under a protected shelter. He was too old and fragile at that point to go safariing. Fritzi and I were treated to a wonderful, close-up celebration of monitor lizards, antelopes, giraffes, okapis, bongo, apes of all shapes, and infant twin pygmy hippos who sucked our thumbs. I was in animal heaven. What a glorious day. A combination of two of my great loves in one afternoon. Animals and the Franks. Never tell me dreams can't come true.

That evening some of the Franks' friends and family stopped by. I met Otto's diminutive, adorable "little" sister, Leni (in her eighties!). The tiny bundle of nerves and wit, still very pretty, was the mother of Buddy. Full of energy, always in motion, she was still a prosperous antiques dealer, as she had been most of her life. I flashed on Anne. This peppery little lady was yet another extension of the feisty, brilliant niece. I was seeing and understanding the many-faceted teenager's roots.

The group of people who gathered into the Frank's cozy front room were all in their late sixties, seventies, and early eighties, but I had never met a group of senior citizens like them before. They were dynamic, teasing, vivacious, very much filled with life and self-esteem. They spoke in rapid German, hands wildly gesticulating, stopping only to briefly translate for me. The gist of their conversation between talk of vacations and theater and mutual friends was their fury over the new generation of Germans.

The group spoke of a growing, terrifying neo-Nazi movement. It taught this new generation that the concentration camps and six million dead Jews were all Jewish propaganda. It never happened. The movement professed that Hitler was a redeemer—a great German leader—and anything that challenged his revered reputation was simply a lie. And Anne Frank's *The Diary of a Young Girl* was the greatest lie of all. Pure fiction. I was sick. It couldn't be true what these people were telling me. They must be exaggerating. But something inside told me they were not.

Our last day together is etched so clearly in my memory. We sat outside on the little patio. The smell of flowers filled the air: sweet peas and morning dew grass and the Anne Frank roses.

Otto opened the door and sat down next to me. He had brought out a whole pile of notebooks and a small, red-and-white checked diary. I gasped.

"This is not the real diary, Cara, it is a duplicate—an exact replica of the original. The real one is in the bank in a safe. But this one is put together exactly like Anne's. I have taped every little paper just the way she did. We had to be frugal with paper, you know. So Anne wrote on any scrap she could get her hands on."

I turned each page slowly, examined the graceful Dutch script, and saw how she changed her signature after many passages. She had been experimenting: "Anna M. Frank," "A.M. Frank," "Anna Marie Frank." There was a sketch. A skating dress that she had envisioned herself wearing when she and cousin Buddy would skate their duet. There was much writing along the borders. Otto told me it was her comments: "I do not feel this way now, but I did then so I won't change it."

And then Otto told me something that amazes me still: Anne had actually rewritten her diary. She had a sort of premonition that her words could very well live on after her. This idea came to her after listening to the radio. The commentator, Bolkestein, had said how fascinating it would be to someday gather all the diaries of all the Jews in hiding after the war and discover what their lives had been like. That hit a note with the young girl.

> . . . my greatest wish is to become a journalist someday and later on a famous writer. Whether these leanings towards greatness (or insanity?) will ever materialize remains to be seen, but I certainly have the subjects in mind. In any case, I want to publish a book entitled Het Achterhuis ("the house behind," translated from Dutch) after the war. Whether I shall succeed or not, I cannot say, but my diary will be a great help . . . (Anne, The Diary)

So she began editing her diary, refining her writing. Otto emphasized that she never changed the message of each passage, but would only perfect the writing so it would read better.

Along with her almost daily entries, she had also rewritten her earlier observations into four packed notebooks. The original diary is written to not only "Dear Kitty" (a favored friend), but to other special friends as well. The rewritten diary sticks to only Kitty. She also stopped playing around with various sign-offs. She had decided on a simple, "Yours, Anne." She wanted a continuity. No confusion. A flow of thought. She even censored herself, thinking that some passages would be entirely too boring.

Otto put many of those extracted passages right back into the published diary, particularly those dealing with her love for Peter. He felt that young people would greatly identify with this kind of pain, called "growing up." Anything too intimate he left out.

I looked at the thick notebooks and my awe for this vibrant spirit, this very old-beyond-her-years teen tripled. Within that tiny sequestered apartment she wrote and rewrote one of the greatest works of art in history. She wrote stories. She invented games. Even made up a secret language. She was keeping herself alive. And she was a liberated woman decades before any of us were.

I want to get on; I can't imagine that I would have to lead the same sort of life as Mummy and Mrs. Van Daan and all the women who do their work and are then forgotten. I must have something besides a husband and children, something that I can devote myself to!

I want to go on living even after my death! And therefore I am grateful to God for giving me this gift, this possibility of developing myself and of writing, of expressing all that is in me. (*Anne,* The Diary)

(Today, the unabridged diary is available to the public under the title, *The Diary of Anne Frank: The Critical Edition.*)

"Otto," I asked, "did you know Anne was so creative, so sensitive?" The question saddened him.

"I did not know that side of Anne. She never let any of us know that side of her. I would have expected her sister, Margot, to have such depth of emotion, but Anne . . . she was so temperamental, so private, so very funny. No, Cara, I did not know my child."

The Gemini teenager would write:

> *I've already told you before that I have, as it were, a dual personality. One half embodies my exuberant cheerfulness, making fun of everything, my high-spiritedness, and above all the way I take everything lightly. This includes not taking offense at a flirtation, a kiss, an embrace, a dirty joke. This side is usually lying in wait and pushes away the other which is much better, deeper and purer. You must realize that no one knows Anne's better side and that's why most people find me so insufferable.* (*Anne*, The Diary)

It took Otto months and months of time and draining emotion to get through the writings of his dead daughter. When he had compiled a completed manuscript, he sent a copy to his mother. Other people read the work, and finally Otto was urged by his friends to let it be published. The world must know about Anne Frank.

I looked at the old man thumbing through the pages of the little checked diary (which represents only a fragment of Anne's writings). How very much like her father Anne must have been. She seemed to have resembled him as well. The slightly protruding front teeth, the shy smile, the handsome, striking features, the quick sense of humor, the sparkling, penetrating eyes. Anne Frank's father was looking through her diary, and I took a picture so I would never forget. It appears on the front cover of this book.

Later, while Otto napped and Fritzi cleaned her kitchen, I gathered Anne's short stories around me and read a few of them before I fell into a dreamy sleep on the patio. I had never felt her presence so strongly. It was a growing moment for me. I realized I was not Anne Frank reincarnated, as I think I quietly wanted to believe. I was not her. Wasn't brilliant like her. Wasn't doomed to die. Not just yet. I was still alive. And, maybe for the first time, happy to be *me*.

Being so close to Anne's ink impressions, next to the man she so lovingly called "Pim," who looked more like her than me, helped to focus my attention forward. I couldn't resurrect her. I couldn't adopt Otto. But I could get on with my life. An idea that Anne—and her father—had expressed so eloquently.

At the tram station, I turned to Fritzi. Otto was resting across the room. "Fritzi, does it bother you that people react so strongly to Otto? So many times, because of Anne, he is the focus of attention. Do you ever feel upstaged?"

Fritzi looked so poignant, so earnest. Her face softened into a glow—this strong, kind, elegant woman whose face has known much more sorrow than laughter.

"Oh no, Cara. My whole life is for Otto. I love to help him, work along with him. There is nothing I want to do more in all the world."

I hugged her. I knew that it was this woman who had helped Otto to live again. Helped him answer the incredible letters pouring into them from around the world. Helped him feel joy in the constant reminders of his joyless past.

I looked at my darling Otto sitting so straight and serious. I wanted to remember every word he spoke, every touch. How he would stroke my hair. Pat my hand. Say over and over again as we toured briefly the ancient streets of Basel, "We can't see everything. Just a little, just a little."

And I would remember always his face as he told me quietly, "It was good that you came now, Cara. I'm a very old man, you know."

The last time I saw him I was staring back from inside the tram. As it pulled out of the station, he was standing so tall on the platform, his strong, sweet lady by his side.

She waved in my direction, and he clasped his hands together and swayed ever so gently toward me: a Jew at prayer. And I saw there were tears in his eyes, too.

Epilogue

Our letters continued for two more years until August of 1980, when Otto Frank died. Fritzi wrote me:

> Dearest Cara,
>
> Now my darling Otto has left me and all his friends in the world. Though I know that he wanted to die after his long and fulfilled life with the many sad but also happy events, I miss him terribly. I am glad however that you still saw him when he was his own lovable self. Luckily he did not suffer and passed away peacefully. . . .

This book was one of the hardest challenges I've had to face. For all of my efforts are working on the *now,* and everything in this work is in the *then,* where I truly didn't want to go.

It is a book of reminders, of ghosts—of a house, a marriage, a cozy, secure world that is no longer mine. Change, I have come to understand, is an integral part of life, and though Kent and I will always remain dear friends, we are not marriage partners. The constant is the deep bond with my sons, Ethan and Jesse—now young men—and my many other loved ones, family and friends, around the globe.

Change, as this book reflects, is keenly apparent in every

decade. Along with Otto, Miep's Jan has also died; my Dutch friends who greeted me in Amsterdam, Ellen and Girard, are divorced; my sister's husband, Eli, has been replaced by Dan—her husband of many years and father of Noah and Tess; that "small" agency I referred to, Chiat-Day, is now one of the most powerful in the world.

But in the book, I didn't change Otto's charming syntax, or his proclivity for calling Kent "Ken." I left in my own heady sentences, hopes and dreams, humor and pain. I left Cara as she was then.

This book has forced me to watch myself grow up. An overexuberant, ever-dramatic child. And, as Anne expressed in her diary, I felt a lot of ways then that I don't feel now. I spoke of the need to hate, and I don't feel that now.

Love is the answer for every situation. And that's not New Age airy fairy crystal babble.

But what has never changed is my love for Otto Frank. He took my hand and walked me from childhood to adulthood, as he did for young people all over this world. In our loneliest, angriest, most futile times this grandfather-of-all—this amazing Holocaust survivor—embraced us and loved us unconditionally. And he helped us believe in planting new hopes when the old ones withered and died. As I am doing today. Otto would be happy. . . .